The Psalms Project Volume Nine

Discovering the Spiritual World through the Psalms – Psalm 81-90

Michael Harvey Koplitz

All Scripture quotations, unless otherwise noted, are taken from the New American Standard Bible®, Copyright © 1960, 1962, 1963, 1968, 1971, 1972, 1973, 1975, 1977, 1995 by the Lockman Foundation. Used by permission (www.Lockman.org)

The NASB uses italic to indicate words that have been added for clarification. Citations are shown with large capital letters.

TABLE OF CONTENTS

The goal of this project:

This research project will examine the 150 psalms for the spiritual awareness each Psalm offers. Each Psalm will be examined by its language and the commentary of the Sages. The spiritual awareness analysis will be done in alignment with Ari's definition of the Tree of life, the Book of Creation, and the Zohar. Each verse of the Psalm will be rewritten using the intent of the language and spiritual commentary to convey its spiritual lesson.

The main resources:

The Zohar

The Book of Creation

Ari's writing on the Tree of Life and the Ten Sefirot

The Theological Wordbook of the Old Testament

Samson Hirsch's commentary on the Psalms

Tehillim – Psalms – A new translation with a commentary anthologized from the Talmudic and rabbinic sources

Accordance Bible Software

Psalm 81

New American Standard 1995	Hebrew
Psa. 81:0 For the choir director; 'on the Gittith. *A Psalm* of Asaph.	לַמְנַצֵּחַ ׀ עַל־הַגִּתִּית **Psa. 81:1**
Psa. 81:1 [a]Sing for joy to God our [b]strength; Shout [c]joyfully to the [d]God of Jacob.	לְאָסָף׃ 2 הַרְנִינוּ לֵאלֹהִים עוּזֵּנוּ
2 Raise a song, strike [a]the timbrel, The sweet sounding [b]lyre with the [c]harp.	הָרִיעוּ לֵאלֹהֵי יַעֲקֹב׃ 3 שְׂאוּ־זִמְרָה
3 Blow the trumpet at the [a]new moon, At the full moon, on our [b]feast day.	וּתְנוּ־תֹף כִּנּוֹר נָעִים עִם־נָבֶל׃ 4
4 For it is a statute for Israel, An ordinance of the God of Jacob.	תִּקְעוּ בַחֹדֶשׁ שׁוֹפָר בַּכֶּסֶה לְיוֹם
5 He established it for a testimony in Joseph When he [1][a]went throughout the land of Egypt. I heard a [b]language that I did not know:	חַגֵּנוּ׃ 5 כִּי חֹק לְיִשְׂרָאֵל הוּא מִשְׁפָּט לֵאלֹהֵי יַעֲקֹב׃ 6 עֵדוּת ׀ בִּיהוֹסֵף שָׂמוֹ בְּצֵאתוֹ עַל־אֶרֶץ מִצְרָיִם שְׂפַת לֹא־יָדַעְתִּי אֶשְׁמָע׃ 7 הֲסִירוֹתִי מִסֵּבֶל שִׁכְמוֹ כַּפָּיו מִדּוּד תַּעֲבֹרְנָה׃ 8 בַּצָּרָה קָרָאתָ וָאֲחַלְּצֶךָּ אֶעֶנְךָ בְּסֵתֶר רַעַם אֶבְחָנְךָ עַל־מֵי מְרִיבָה סֶלָה׃ 9 שְׁמַע עַמִּי וְאָעִידָה בָּךְ יִשְׂרָאֵל אִם־תִּשְׁמַע־לִי׃ 10 לֹא־ יִהְיֶה בְךָ אֵל זָר וְלֹא תִשְׁתַּחֲוֶה לְאֵל נֵכָר׃ 11 אָנֹכִי ׀ יְהוָה אֱלֹהֶיךָ הַמַּעַלְךָ מֵאֶרֶץ מִצְרָיִם הַרְחֶב־פִּיךָ
Psa. 81:6 "I [1][a]relieved his shoulder of the burden, His hands were freed from the [2]basket.	וַאֲמַלְאֵהוּ׃ 12 וְלֹא־שָׁמַע עַמִּי לְקוֹלִי וְיִשְׂרָאֵל לֹא־אָבָה לִי׃ 13
7 "You [a]called in trouble and I rescued you; I [b]answered you in the hiding place of thunder;	וָאֲשַׁלְּחֵהוּ בִּשְׁרִירוּת לִבָּם יֵלְכוּ בְּמוֹעֲצוֹתֵיהֶם׃ 14 לוּ עַמִּי שֹׁמֵעַ לִי יִשְׂרָאֵל בִּדְרָכַי יְהַלֵּכוּ׃ 15 כִּמְעַט אוֹיְבֵיהֶם אַכְנִיעַ וְעַל צָרֵיהֶם אָשִׁיב יָדִי׃ 16 מְשַׂנְאֵי יְהוָה יְכַחֲשׁוּ־לוֹ וִיהִי עִתָּם לְעוֹלָם׃ 17 וַיַּאֲכִילֵהוּ

I proved you at the [c]waters of Meribah.   [1]Selah.

8   "[a]Hear, O My people, and I will [1]admonish you;

O Israel, if you [b]would listen to Me!

9   "Let there be no [a]strange god among you;

Nor shall you worship any foreign god.

10   "[a]I, the LORD, am your God,

Who brought you up from the land of Egypt;

[b]Open your mouth wide and I will [c]fill it.

Psa. 81:11   "But My people [a]did not listen to My voice,

And Israel did not [1]obey Me.

12   "So I [a]gave [1]them over to the stubbornness of their heart,

To walk in their own devices.

13   "Oh that My people [a]would listen to Me,

That Israel would [b]walk in My ways!

14   "I would quickly [a]subdue their enemies

And [b]turn My hand against tr adversaries.

15   "[a]Those who hate the LORD would [b]pretend obedience to Him,

And their time *of punishment* would be forever.

16   "[1]But I would feed you with the [2a]finest of the wheat,

מֵחֵלֶב חִטָּה וּמִצּוּר דְּבַשׁ
אַשְׂבִּיעֶךָ :

And with [b]honey from the rock I would satisfy you."	

References

Psalm 81:0
[†]Or *according to*

Psalm 81:1
[a]Ps 51:14; 59:16; 95:1
[b]Ps 46:1
Ps 66:1; 95:2; 98:4
[d]Ps 84:8

Psalm 81:2
[a]Ex 15:20; Ps 149:3
[b]Ps 92:3; 98:5; 147:7
Ps 108:2; 144:9

Psalm 81:3
[a]Num 10:10
[b]Lev 23:24

Psalm 81:5
[1]Lit *went out over*
[a]Ex 11:4
[b]Deut 28:49; Ps 114:1; Jer 5:15

Psalm 81:6
[1]Lit *removed his shoulder from*
[2]Or *brick load*
[a]Is 9:4; 10:27

Psalm 81:7
[1]*Selah* may mean: *Pause, Crescendo* or *Musical interlude*
[a]Ex 2:23; 14:10; Ps 50:15
[b]Ex 19:19; 20:18
Ex 17:6, 7; Num 20:13; Ps 95:8

Psalm 81:8
[1]Or *bear witness against*
[a]Ps 50:7

[b]Ps 95:7

Psalm 81:9
[a]Ex 20:3; Deut 5:7; 32:12; Ps 44:20; Is 43:12

Psalm 81:10
[a]Ex 20:2; Deut 5:6
[b]Job 29:23
[c]Ps 37:4; 78:25; 107:9

Psalm 81:11
[1]Lit *yield to*
[a]Deut 32:15; Ps 106:25

Psalm 81:12
[1]Lit *him*
[a]Job 8:4; Acts 7:42; Rom 1:24, 26

Psalm 81:13
[a]Deut 5:29; Ps 81:8; Is 48:18
[b]Ps 128:1; Is 42:24; Jer 7:23

Psalm 81:14
[a]Ps 18:47; 47:3
[b]Amos 1:8

Psalm 81:15
[a]Rom 1:30
[b]Ps 18:44; 66:3

Psalm 81:16
[1]Lit *He would feed him*
[2]Lit *fat*
[a]Deut 32:14; Ps 147:14
[b]Deut 32:13

Targum

Psa. 81:1 For praise; on the lyre that comes from Gath, composed by Asaph. ² Give praise in the presence of God, our strength; shout in the presence of the God of Jacob. ³ Lift up the voice in praise, and set out timbrels, the lyre whose sound is sweet with harps. ⁴ Blow the horn in the month of Tishri, in the month in which the day of our festivals is concealed. ⁵ For he made a covenant for Israel; it is a legal ruling of the God of Jacob. ⁶ He made it a testimony for Joseph, who did not go near the wife of his master; on that day he went out of the prison and ruled over all the land of Egypt. The tongue I did not know I have taught [and] heard. ⁷ I have removed his shoulder from servitude; his hands were taken away from casting clay into a pot. ⁸ In the time of the distress of Egypt, you called and I delivered you; I made you fast in the secret place where my presence is, where wheels of fire call out before him; I tested you by the waters of Dispute forever. ⁹ Hear, O my people, and I will bear witness for you, O Israel, if you will accept my word. ¹⁰ There shall not be among you worshippers of a foreign idol, and you shall not bow down to a profane idol. ¹¹ I am the LORD your God, who brought you up from the land of Egypt; open wide your mouth with the words of Torah, and I will fill it with all good things. ¹² But my people did not receive my voice; and Israel did not want my word. ¹³ And I expelled them for the thoughts of their heart, they went away in their wicked counsel. ¹⁴ Would that my people had listened to me – that Israel would walk in my ways! ¹⁵ In a little while I will humble their enemies, and I will turn my strong blow against their enemies. ¹⁶ The enemies of the LORD will be false to him; and their harshness will last forever. ¹⁷ But he will feed him with the best of wheat bread; and I will satisfy you with honey from the rock.

Spiritual Awareness

Introduction

In this Psalm, Israel beseeched the LORD to free His people from their Babylonian Exile. This Psalm celebrates the divine salvation which ended Israel's servitude in Egypt. The process of Egyptian salvation started six months earlier on the first day of Tishrei, Rosh HaShannah, when the Israelites stopped working as slaves for the Egyptian taskmasters (from Rosh Hashanah 11a of the Talmud). This Psalm was designated to accompany the Temple sacrifices on Rosh Hashanah (from Rosh Hashanah 30b of the Talmud).

Superscript

The meaning of the Hebrew word הַגִּתִּית is unknown. This Psalm visualizes the splendor of which grapes. Rabbi Hirsch believes this word means wine-pressing or some part of the process.

To the Sefirah Netzach who grants victory, upon the "wine pressing" by Asaf.

Verse one

The phrase "God of Jacob" raises the speculation that the Psalmist knew Israel followed the LORD's Laws of the Torah. However, like Jacob, they got into the gray areas and perhaps crossed the line in a few ways. Jacob was a trickster in that he fooled his brother Esau into giving him the birthright and the blessing of their father, Isaac. The Psalmist is reminding Israel that they have been tricksters before the LORD.

Stir up jubilation to God, our strength; waken homage to the God of Jacob.

Verse three

This verse refers to the holy day of Rosh Hashanah.

But blow the shofar at the New Moon on the day of the veiling of the moon for the day of our festival.

Verse five

The people were to emulate Joseph, who remained faithful to the LORD's spiritual and moral truth and purity even in the face of a godless nation. The exiled people needed to stay loyal to the LORD while exiled in Babylon.

He had appointed it in Joseph as a testimony when He went forth over the land of Egypt; I shall henceforth hear the speech of one Whom I had not known before.

Verse seven

The waters of Meribah are the waters of contention.

You called in distress, and I have made you free; so I shall answer you even hidden in thunder; I shall test you at the Waters of Contention. Meditate on this verse.

Verse nine

An "alien god" or "foreign god" was a god who was served by the Gentile nations. The Psalmist warns the people of Israel, even in exile, they must not allow the culture that surrounded them to penetrate them. The gods of Babylon must never replace the LORD.

There shall be no alien god within you, nor shall you prostrate yourself before a foreign god.

Psalm 82

New American Standard 1995	Hebrew

Psa. 82:0   A Psalm of Asaph.

Psa. 82:1   God takes His *a*stand in [1]His own congregation;

He *b*judges in the midst of the [2c]rulers.

[2]   How long will you *a*judge unjustly
And *b*show partiality to the wicked?
[1]Selah.

[3]   *a*Vindicate the weak and fatherless;
Do justice to the afflicted and destitute.

[4]   *a*Rescue the weak and needy;
Deliver *them* out of the hand of the wicked.

Psa. 82:5   They *a*do not know nor do they understand;

They *b*walk about in darkness;

All the *c*foundations of the earth are shaken.

[6]   [1]I *a*said, "You are gods,
And all of you are *b*sons of the Most High.

[7]   "Nevertheless *a*you will die like men
And fall like *any* *b*one of the princes."

[8]   *a*Arise, O God, *b*judge the earth!
For it is You who *c*possesses all the nations.

מִזְמוֹר לְאָסָף אֱלֹהִים נִצָּב **Psa. 82:1**

בַּעֲדַת־אֵל בְּקֶרֶב אֱלֹהִים יִשְׁפֹּט ׃ [2]

עַד־מָתַי תִּשְׁפְּטוּ־עָוֶל וּפְנֵי רְשָׁעִים

תִּשְׂאוּ־סֶלָה ׃ [3] שִׁפְטוּ־דַל וְיָתוֹם

עָנִי וָרָשׁ הַצְדִּיקוּ ׃ [4] פַּלְּטוּ־דַל

וְאֶבְיוֹן מִיַּד רְשָׁעִים הַצִּילוּ ׃ [5] לֹא

יָדְעוּ וְלֹא יָבִינוּ בַּחֲשֵׁכָה יִתְהַלָּכוּ

יִמּוֹטוּ כָּל־מוֹסְדֵי אָרֶץ ׃ [6] אֲנִי־

אָמַרְתִּי אֱלֹהִים אַתֶּם וּבְנֵי עֶלְיוֹן

כֻּלְּכֶם ׃ [7] אָכֵן כְּאָדָם תְּמוּתוּן

וּכְאַחַד הַשָּׂרִים תִּפֹּלוּ ׃ [8] קוּמָה

אֱלֹהִים שָׁפְטָה הָאָרֶץ כִּי־אַתָּה

תִנְחַל בְּכָל־הַגּוֹיִם ׃

References

Psalm 82:1
[1]Lit *the congregation of God*
[2]Lit *gods*
[a]Is 3:13
[b]2 Chr 19:6; Ps 58:11
[c]Ex 21:6; 22:8, 28

Psalm 82:2
[1]*Selah* may mean: *Pause, Crescendo* or *Musical interlude*
[a]Ps 58:1
[b]Deut 1:17; Prov 18:5

Psalm 82:3
[a]Deut 24:17; Ps 10:18; Is 11:4; Jer 22:16

Psalm 82:4
[a]Job 29:12

Psalm 82:5
[a]Ps 14:4; Jer 4:22; Mic 3:1
[b]Prov 2:13; Is 59:9; Jer 23:12
[c]Ps 11:3

Psalm 82:6
[1]Lit *I, on my part*
[a]Ps 82:1; John 10:34
[b]Ps 89:26

Psalm 82:7
[a]Job 21:32; Ps 49:12; Ezek 31:14
[b]Ps 83:11

Psalm 82:8
[a]Ps 12:5

[b]Ps 58:11; 96:13
[c]Ps 2:8; Rev 11:15

Targum

Psa. 82:1 A hymn composed by Asaph. God, his presence abides in the assembly of the righteous who are strong in Torah; he will give judgment in the midst of the righteous judges. ² How long, O wicked, will you judge falsely, and lift up the faces of the wicked forever? ³ Judge the poor and the orphan; acquit the needy and the poor. ⁴ Save the poor and needy, from the hands of the wicked deliver them. ⁵ They do not know how to do good, and they do not understand the Torah, they walk in darkness; because of this, the pillars of the earth's foundations shake. ⁶ I said, "You are reckoned as angels, and all of you are like angels of the height." ⁷ But truly you will die like the sons of men; and like one of the leaders you will fall. ⁸ Arise, O LORD, judge all the inhabitants of the earth; for you will possess all the Gentiles.

Spiritual Awareness

Introduction

This Psalm is a vigorous affirmation of the Torah judicial system and a forceful condemnation of persons who try to corrupt the LORD's Laws. The Talmud, Rosh Hashanah 31a), designates this as the "Song of the Day" for the third day of the week. This is because, on the third day of Creation, the LORD uncovered the earth with His wisdom. This alludes to Genesis 1:9, where the LORD allowed the water to reveal land.

The sage Maharsha explained that the earth's continued existence depends on maintaining equity and justice. In the Pirkei Avos (Ethics of the Fathers 1:10), we learn that the world endures because of truth, justice, and peace. In the Talmud Shabbos 10a, every judge who renders true justice becomes a partner of the LORD in the work of Creation.

Superscript and verse one

There is nothing that reveals the LORD more clearly as the founder and maintainer of human society than justice which was ingrained into the spirit and conscience of man at the time of Creation.

A Psalm of Asaf. God stands in every tribunal of God; He judges in the midst of the judges.

Verse two

How long will you enforce violence in your judgment and respect the persons of the lawless? Meditate on this verse.

Psalm 83

New American Standard 1995	Hebrew
Psa. 83:0 A Song, a Psalm of Asaph.	שִׁיר מִזְמוֹר לְאָסָף : **Psa. 83:1** ²
Psa. 83:1 O God, [a]do not remain quiet;	אֱלֹהִים אַל־דֳּמִי־לָךְ אַל־תֶּחֱרַשׁ
[b]Do not be silent and, O God, do not be still.	וְאַל־תִּשְׁקֹט אֵל : ³ כִּי־הִנֵּה אוֹיְבֶיךָ
2 For behold, Your enemies [a]make an uproar,	יֶהֱמָיוּן וּמְשַׂנְאֶיךָ נָשְׂאוּ רֹאשׁ : ⁴
And [b]those who hate You have [1c]exalted themselves.	עַל־עַמְּךָ יַעֲרִימוּ סוֹד וְיִתְיָעֲצוּ
3 They [a]make shrewd plans against Your people,	עַל־צְפוּנֶיךָ : ⁵ אָמְרוּ לְכוּ וְנַכְחִידֵם
And [1]conspire together against [b]Your [2]treasured ones.	מִגּוֹי וְלֹא־יִזָּכֵר שֵׁם־יִשְׂרָאֵל עוֹד : ⁶
4 They have said, "Come, and [d]let us wipe them out [1]as a nation,	כִּי נוֹעֲצוּ לֵב יַחְדָּו עָלֶיךָ בְּרִית
That the [b]name of Israel be remembered no more."	יִכְרֹתוּ : ⁷ אָהֳלֵי אֱדוֹם וְיִשְׁמְעֵאלִים
5 For they have [1a]conspired together with one mind;	מוֹאָב וְהַגְרִים : ⁸ גְּבָל וְעַמּוֹן
Against You they make a covenant:	וַעֲמָלֵק פְּלֶשֶׁת עִם־יֹשְׁבֵי צוֹר : ⁹
6 The tents of [a]Edom and the [b]Ishmaelites,	גַּם־אַשּׁוּר נִלְוָה עִמָּם הָיוּ זְרוֹעַ
[c]Moab and the [d]Hagrites;	לִבְנֵי־לוֹט סֶלָה : ¹⁰ עֲשֵׂה־לָהֶם
7 [a]Gebal and [b]Ammon and [c]Amalek,	כְּמִדְיָן כְּסִיסְרָא כְיָבִין בְּנַחַל
[d]Philistia with the inhabitants of [e]Tyre;	קִישׁוֹן : ¹¹ נִשְׁמְדוּ בְעֵין־דֹּאר הָיוּ
8 [a]Assyria also has joined with them;	דֹּמֶן לָאֲדָמָה : ¹² שִׁיתֵמוֹ נְדִיבֵמוֹ
They have become [1]a help to the [b]children of Lot. [2]Selah.	כְּעֹרֵב וְכִזְאֵב וּכְזֶבַח וּכְצַלְמֻנָּע
	כָּל־נְסִיכֵמוֹ : ¹³ אֲשֶׁר אָמְרוּ נִירֲשָׁה
	לָּנוּ אֵת נְאוֹת אֱלֹהִים : ¹⁴ אֱלֹהַי
Psa. 83:9 Deal with them [a]as with Midian,	שִׁיתֵמוֹ כַגַּלְגַּל כְּקַשׁ לִפְנֵי־רוּחַ : ¹⁵
	כְּאֵשׁ תִּבְעַר־יָעַר וּכְלֶהָבָה תְּלַהֵט
	הָרִים : ¹⁶ כֵּן תִּרְדְּפֵם בְּסַעֲרֶךָ
	וּבְסוּפָתְךָ תְבַהֲלֵם : ¹⁷ מַלֵּא פְנֵיהֶם
	קָלוֹן וִיבַקְשׁוּ שִׁמְךָ יְהוָה : ¹⁸ יֵבֹשׁוּ

As [b]with Sisera *and* Jabin at the torrent of Kishon,

10 Who were destroyed at En-dor,

Who [a]became as dung for the ground.

11 Make their nobles like [a]Oreb and Zeeb

And all their princes like [b]Zebah and Zalmunna,

12 Who said, "[a]Let us possess for ourselves

The [b]pastures of God."

Psa. 83:13 O my God, make them like the [1a]whirling dust,

Like [b]chaff before the wind.

14 Like [a]fire that burns the forest

And like a flame that [b]sets the mountains on fire,

15 So pursue them [a]with Your tempest

And terrify them with Your storm.

16 [a]Fill their faces with dishonor,

That they may seek Your name, O LORD.

17 Let them be [a]ashamed and dismayed forever,

And let them be humiliated and perish,

18 That they may [a]know that [b]You alone, whose name is the LORD,

Are the [c]Most High over all the earth.

וַיִּבָּהֲלוּ עֲדֵי־עַד וְיַחְפְּרוּ וְיֹאבֵדוּ ׃

19 וְיֵדְעוּ כִּי־אַתָּה שִׁמְךָ יְהוָה לְבַדֶּךָ עֶלְיוֹן עַל־כָּל־הָאָרֶץ ׃

References

Psalm 83:1
[a]Ps 28:1; 35:22
[b]Ps 109:1

Psalm 83:2
[1]Lit *lifted up the head*
[a]Ps 2:1; Is 17:12
[b]Ps 81:15
[c]Judg 8:28; Zech 1:21

Psalm 83:3
[1]Or *consult*
[2]Or *hidden ones*
[a]Ps 64:2; Is 29:15
[b]Ps 27:5; 31:20

Psalm 83:4
[1]Lit *from*
[a]Esth 3:6; Ps 74:8; Jer 48:2
[b]Ps 41:5; Jer 11:19

Psalm 83:5
[1]Or *consulted*
[a]Ps 2:2; Dan 6:7

Psalm 83:6
[a]2 Chr 20:10; Ps 137:7
[b]Gen 25:12-16
[c]2 Chr 20:10
[d]1 Chr 5:10

Psalm 83:7
[a]Josh 13:5; Ezek 27:9
[b]2 Chr 20:10
[c]1 Sam 15:2
[d]1 Sam 4:1; 29:1
[e]Ezek 27:3; Amos 1:9

Psalm 83:8
[1]Lit *an arm*
[2]*Selah* may mean: *Pause, Crescendo* or *Musical interlude*
[a]2 Kin 15:19
[b]Deut 2:9

Psalm 83:9
[a]Judg 7:1-24
[b]Judg 4:7, 15, 21-24

Psalm 83:10
[a]Zeph 1:17

Psalm 83:11
[a]Judg 7:25
[b]Judg 8:12, 21

Psalm 83:12
[a]2 Chr 20:11
[b]Ps 132:13

Psalm 83:13
[1]Or *tumbleweed*
[a]Is 17:13
[b]Job 21:18; Ps 35:5; Is 40:24; Jer 13:24

Psalm 83:14
[a]Is 9:18
[b]Ex 19:18; Deut 32:22

Psalm 83:15
[a]Job 9:17; Ps 58:9

Psalm 83:16
[a]Job 10:15; Ps 109:29; 132:18

Psalm 83:17
[a]Ps 35:4; 70:2

Psalm 83:18
[a]Ps 59:13

[b]Ps 86:10; Is 45:21
[c]Ps 9:2; 18:13; 97:9

Targum

Psa. 83:1 A song and Psalm composed by Asaph. [2] God, do not become silent; do not be uncaring, and do not be quiet, O God. [3] For, behold, your enemies are stirred up, and your foes have lifted their head. [4] Against your people they have contrived a secret plan, and they take counsel together against things hidden in your treasuries. [5] They say, "Come, let us conceal them from being a people, and the name of Israel will not be mentioned again." [6] For they take counsel together against you with all their heart, and make a covenant on your account. [7] The tents of the Edomites and Arabs, the Moabites and Hungarites. [8] The Gublites and Ammonites and Amalekites, the Philistines with the inhabitants of Tyre. [9] Also Sennacherib, king of Assyria, allied himself with them; they became a support for the sons of Lot forever. [10] Do to them as you did to Midian, to Sisera, and as you did to Jabin at the stream of Kishon. [11] They were destroyed at the spring of Dor; they were as dung that is trampled on the earth. [12] Make them and their chiefs like Oreb and like Zeeb; and all their kings like Zeba and Zalmunna. [13] Who had said, "We will inherit for ourselves all the fields of the god Elohim." [14] O my God, make them like a wheel that keeps on rolling and does not stop, down a slope; and like straw before a storm. [15] Like fire that burns in the forest, and like the flame that ignites the plants of the mountains. [16] Thus will you pursue them with your storm wind, and you will frighten them with your gale. [17] Fill their faces with shame, and they will seek your name, O LORD. [18] They will be ashamed and terrified for ages upon ages; and they will be disgraced and will perish. [19] And they will know that you, your name the LORD, are alone supreme over all the inhabitants of the earth.

Spiritual Awareness

Introduction

This Psalm is based on the accomplishments of King Jehoshofat, with can be found in 2 Chronicles. This king renovated the justice system in Judea. Judea was attacked during his reign by the Ammonites, Moabites, Aramites, and Seirites (Edom). The Psalmist reveals the deeper intention of these attacks. These nations not only wanted to destroy Judah, but they also wanted to remove the LORD's name from the earth. Jehoshaphat used the power of song as his chief weapon against his foes. He declared that the LORD does reign over the universe. Judah's survival was the proof.

General notes on Spiritual Awareness in this Psalm

This part of history repeats a theme that is still in use today. With the LORD, anything is possible. Jehoshaphat was outnumbered by the surrounding nations that wanted to destroy Judah. Had that occurred, the name of the LORD and His presence would have been lost upon the earth forever? Perhaps that is too powerful a statement. It is unknown if the LORD would have tried to find another Chosen People. However, the LORD had a covenant with Abraham that his descendants would always be maintained. At least a remnant of the people would always survive. Therefore, as long as Judah lived by the Ten Commandments and the Torah, the LORD would be with them. During Jehoshaphat's reign, he brought the nation back from idolatry to following the ways of the LORD. Therefore, when the attacks came, the LORD was with Judah, and the LORD proved to the world that there was one supreme God. Monotheism was only a part of Hebraic culture at that time. Therefore, the nations who attacked Judah believed their god was inferior to the God of Israel.

Psalm 84

New American Standard 1995	Hebrew

Psa. 84:0 For the choir director; †on the Gittith. A Psalm of the sons of Korah.
 	
Psa. 84:1 How lovely are Your *a*dwelling places,
    O LORD of hosts!
2   My *a*soul longed and even yearned for the courts of the LORD;
    My heart and my flesh sing for joy to the *b*living God.
3   The bird also has found a house, And the swallow a nest for herself, where she may lay her young, Even Your *a*altars, O LORD of hosts,
    *b*My King and my God.
4   How *a*blessed are those who dwell in Your house!
    They are *b*ever praising You. ¹Selah.
 	
Psa. 84:5 How blessed is the man whose *a*strength is in You, In ¹whose heart are the *b*highways *to Zion!*
6   Passing through the valley of ¹Baca they make it a ²spring; The *a*early rain also covers it with blessings.
7   They *a*go from strength to strength, ¹*Every one of them* *b*appears before God in Zion.
 	
Psa. 84:8 O *a*LORD God of hosts, hear my prayer;
	לַמְנַצֵּחַ עַל־הַגִּתִּית לִבְנֵי־ **Psa. 84:1**
	קֹרַח מִזְמוֹר ׃ ² מַה־יְּדִידוֹת
	מִשְׁכְּנוֹתֶיךָ יְהוָה צְבָאוֹת ׃ ³ נִכְסְפָה
	וְגַם־כָּלְתָה ׀ נַפְשִׁי לְחַצְרוֹת יְהוָה
	לִבִּי וּבְשָׂרִי יְרַנְּנוּ אֶל אֵל־חָי ׃ ⁴
	גַּם־צִפּוֹר ׀ מָצְאָה בַיִת וּדְרוֹר ׀ קֵן
	לָהּ אֲשֶׁר־שָׁתָה אֶפְרֹחֶיהָ אֶת־
	מִזְבְּחוֹתֶיךָ יְהוָה צְבָאוֹת מַלְכִּי
	וֵאלֹהָי ׃ ⁵ אַשְׁרֵי יוֹשְׁבֵי בֵיתֶךָ עוֹד
	יְהַלְלוּךָ סֶּלָה ׃ ⁶ אַשְׁרֵי אָדָם עוֹז־
	לוֹ בָךְ מְסִלּוֹת בִּלְבָבָם ׃ ⁷ עֹבְרֵי ׀
	בְּעֵמֶק הַבָּכָא מַעְיָן יְשִׁיתוּהוּ גַּם־
	בְּרָכוֹת יַעְטֶה מוֹרֶה ׃ ⁸ יֵלְכוּ מֵחַיִל
	אֶל־חָיִל יֵרָאֶה אֶל־אֱלֹהִים בְּצִיּוֹן ׃
	⁹ יְהוָה אֱלֹהִים צְבָאוֹת שִׁמְעָה
	תְפִלָּתִי הַאֲזִינָה אֱלֹהֵי יַעֲקֹב סֶלָה ׃
	¹⁰ מָגִנֵּנוּ רְאֵה אֱלֹהִים וְהַבֵּט פְּנֵי
	מְשִׁיחֶךָ ׃ ¹¹ כִּי טוֹב־יוֹם בַּחֲצֵרֶיךָ
	מֵאָלֶף בָּחַרְתִּי הִסְתּוֹפֵף בְּבֵית
	אֱלֹהַי מִדּוּר בְּאָהֳלֵי־רֶשַׁע ׃ ¹² כִּי
	שֶׁמֶשׁ ׀ וּמָגֵן יְהוָה אֱלֹהִים חֵן
	וְכָבוֹד יִתֵּן יְהוָה לֹא יִמְנַע־טוֹב
	לַהֹלְכִים בְּתָמִים ׃ ¹³ יְהוָה צְבָאוֹת
	אַשְׁרֵי אָדָם בֹּטֵחַ בָּךְ ׃

Give ear, O [b]God of Jacob! Selah.

9   Behold our [a]shield, O God,
And look upon the face of [b]Your anointed.

10   For [a]a day in Your courts is better than a thousand *outside.*
I would rather stand at the threshold of the house of my God
Than dwell in the tents of wickedness.

11   For the LORD God is [a]a sun and [b]shield;
The LORD gives grace and [c]glory;
[d]No good thing does He withhold [1]from those who walk [2]uprightly.

12   O LORD of hosts,
How [a]blessed is the man who trusts in You!

References

Psalm 84:1
[a]Ps 43:3; 132:5

Psalm 84:2
[a]Ps 42:1, 2; 63:1
[b]Ps 42:2

Psalm 84:3
[a]Ps 43:4
[b]Ps 5:2

Psalm 84:4
[1]*Selah* may mean: *Pause, Crescendo* or *Musical interlude*
[a]Ps 65:4
[b]Ps 42:5, 11

Psalm 84:5
[1]Lit *their*
[a]Ps 81:1
[b]Ps 86:11; 122:1; Jer 31:6

Psalm 84:6
[1]Probably, *Weeping;* or *Balsam trees*
[2]Or *place of springs*
[a]Ps 107:35; Joel 2:23

Psalm 84:7
[1]Some ancient versions read *The God of gods will be seen in Zion*
[a]Prov 4:18; Is 40:31; John 1:16; 2 Cor 3:18
[b]Ex 34:23; Deut 16:16; Ps 42:2

Psalm 84:8
[a]Ps 59:5; 80:4; 84:1
[b]Ps 81:1

Psalm 84:9
[a]Gen 15:1; Ps 3:3; 28:7; 59:11; 115:9-11

[b]1 Sam 16:6; 2 Sam 19:21; Ps 2:2; 132:17

Psalm 84:10
[a]Ps 27:4

Psalm 84:11
[1]Lit *with regard to*
[2]Lit *with integrity*
[a]Is 60:19, 20; Mal 4:2; Rev 21:23
[b]Gen 15:1
[c]Ps 85:9
[d]Ps 34:9, 10

Psalm 84:12
[a]Ps 2:12; 40:4

Targum

Psa. 84:1 For praise, on the lyre that comes from Gath; composed by the sons of Korah; a psalm. [2] How beloved are your tents, O LORD Sabaoth! [3] My soul craved and even yearned for the court of the LORD; my heart and flesh meditate on the enduring God. [4] Even the dove has found a house, and the turtledove a nest that is suitable for her hatchlings – to be sacrificed on your altars, O LORD Sabaoth, my king and my God. [5] Happy are the righteous who dwell in your sanctuary; again they will praise you forever. [6] Happy the man who has his strength in your word; trust is in their hearts. [7] The wicked who cross over the valleys of Gehenna, weeping – he will make their weeping like a fountain; also those who return to the teaching of his Torah he will cover with blessings. [8] The righteous go from the sanctuary to the academies; their toil in the Torah will be manifest before the LORD, whose presence abides in Zion. [9] David said, "O LORD, God Sabaoth, receive my prayer; hear, O God of Jacob, forever." [10] See, O God, the merits of our fathers, and behold, the face of your anointed. [11] For it is better to dwell one day in the courtyard of your sanctuary than a thousand in exile; I have chosen to adhere to the sanctuary of God rather than to live in the tents of wickedness. [12] For the LORD God is like a high wall and a strong shield; the LORD will give grace and glory; he will not hide goodness from those who walk in perfection. [13] O LORD Sabaoth, it is well for the son of man who trusts in your word.

Spiritual Awareness

Introduction

This is the first Psalm that was written by the sons of Korach.

"Korach incites a mutiny challenging Moses' leadership and the granting of the *kehunah* (priesthood) to Aaron. He is accompanied by Moses' inveterate foes, Dathan and Abiram. Joining them are 250 distinguished members of the community, who offer the sacrosanct *ketoret* (incense) to prove their worthiness for the priesthood. The earth opens up and swallows the mutineers, and a fire consumes the *ketoret*-offerers."[1]

The sage Radak commented that the Psalm was inspired by King David's experiences when he fled from Saul and entered Philistia. David yearned to return to Israel to see the Ark of the Covenant. David expressed the innermost ongoing of all the lonely exiles in future generations.

Superscript

To the Sefirah Netzach, who grants victory upon the wine pressings. By the sons of Korach, a Psalm.

Verse two

According to the Zohar, 4/5 of the soul is spiritual. The spiritual soul yearns to be close to the LORD. When David was in exile, his soul yearned to be where the LORD was. In his days, the general belief was that the LORD only resided in the land of Israel.

---

[1] "Korach - Parshah - Weekly Torah Portion - Chabad," accessed January 17, 2023, https://www.chabad.org/parshah/default_cdo/aid/45591/jewish/Korach.htm.

My soul yearns; indeed, it pines for the courts of the LORD; my heart and my body sing with joy toward the living God.

Verse four

Forward forever stride those that dwell in Your House; continually they proclaim Your praise. Meditate on this verse.

Verse six

The valley of weeping filled with tears is a metaphor for David's sorrow because he believed he was disconnected from the LORD. When the people of Judah were exiled into the land of Babylon, they felt disconnected from the LORD and longed to return to their homeland.

Wandering through the valley of weeping, they make it into a spring; indeed, into blessings with which a rain envelops.

Verse eight

The phrase "God of Jacob" raises the speculation that the Psalmist knew Israel followed the LORD's Laws of the Torah. However, like Jacob, they got into the gray areas and perhaps crossed the line in a few ways. Jacob was a trickster in fooling his brother Esau into giving him the birthright and the blessing of their father, Isaac. The Psalmist is reminding Israel that they have been tricksters before the LORD.

O God, God of Hosts, hear my prayer; incline your ear, O God of Jacob. Meditate on this verse.

Psalm 85

New American Standard 1995	Hebrew

Psa. 85:0 For the choir director. A Psalm of the sons of Korah.

Psa. 85:1 O LORD, You showed *a*favor to Your land;

You [1]*b*restored the captivity of Jacob.

[2] You *a*forgave the iniquity of Your people;

You *b*covered all their sin. [1]Selah.

[3] You *a*withdrew all Your fury;

You *b*turned away from Your burning anger.

Psa. 85:4 *a*Restore us, O God of our salvation,

And *b*cause Your indignation toward us to cease.

[5] Will *a*You be angry with us forever?

Will You prolong Your anger to [1]all generations?

[6] Will You not Yourself [1]*a*revive us again,

That Your people may *b*rejoice in You?

[7] Show us Your lovingkindness, O LORD,

And *a*grant us Your salvation.

Psa. 85:8 [1]I will hear what God the LORD will say;

For He will *a*speak peace to His people, [2]to His godly ones;

לַמְנַצֵּחַ ׀ לִבְנֵי־קֹרַח **Psa. 85:1**
מִזְמוֹר׃ ² רָצִיתָ יְהוָה אַרְצֶךָ שַׁבְתָּ
שְׁבוּת [שְׁבִית] יַעֲקֹב׃ ³ נָשָׂאתָ עֲוֺן
עַמֶּךָ כִּסִּיתָ כָל־חַטָּאתָם סֶלָה׃ ⁴
אָסַפְתָּ כָל־עֶבְרָתֶךָ הֱשִׁיבוֹתָ
מֵחֲרוֹן אַפֶּךָ׃ ⁵ שׁוּבֵנוּ אֱלֹהֵי יִשְׁעֵנוּ
וְהָפֵר כַּעַסְךָ עִמָּנוּ׃ ⁶ הַלְעוֹלָם
תֶּאֱנַף־בָּנוּ תִּמְשֹׁךְ אַפְּךָ לְדֹר וָדֹר׃
⁷ הֲלֹא־אַתָּה תָּשׁוּב תְּחַיֵּנוּ וְעַמְּךָ
יִשְׂמְחוּ־בָךְ׃ ⁸ הַרְאֵנוּ יְהוָה חַסְדֶּךָ
וְיֶשְׁעֲךָ תִּתֶּן־לָנוּ׃ ⁹ אֶשְׁמְעָה מַה־
יְדַבֵּר הָאֵל ׀ יְהוָה כִּי ׀ יְדַבֵּר
שָׁלוֹם אֶל־עַמּוֹ וְאֶל־חֲסִידָיו וְאַל־
יָשׁוּבוּ לְכִסְלָה׃ ¹⁰ אַךְ ׀ קָרוֹב
לִירֵאָיו יִשְׁעוֹ לִשְׁכֹּן כָּבוֹד
בְּאַרְצֵנוּ׃ ¹¹ חֶסֶד־וֶאֱמֶת נִפְגָּשׁוּ
צֶדֶק וְשָׁלוֹם נָשָׁקוּ׃ ¹² אֱמֶת מֵאֶרֶץ
תִּצְמָח וְצֶדֶק מִשָּׁמַיִם נִשְׁקָף׃ ¹³ גַּם־
יְהוָה יִתֵּן הַטּוֹב וְאַרְצֵנוּ תִּתֵּן
יְבוּלָהּ׃ ¹⁴ צֶדֶק לְפָנָיו יְהַלֵּךְ וְיָשֵׂם
לְדֶרֶךְ פְּעָמָיו׃

But let them not [b]turn back to [3]folly.

9   Surely [a]His salvation is near to those who [1]fear Him,

That [b]glory may dwell in our land.

10   [a]Lovingkindness and [1]truth have met together;

[b]Righteousness and peace have kissed each other.

11   [1]Truth [a]springs from the earth,

And righteousness looks down from heaven.

12   Indeed, [a]the LORD will give what is good,

And our [b]land will yield its produce.

13   [a]Righteousness will go before Him

And will make His footsteps into a way.

References

Psalm 85:1
[1]Or *restore the fortunes*
[a]Ps 77:7; 106:4
[b]Ezra 1:11; Ps 14:7; 126:1; Jer 30:18; Ezek 39:25; Hos 6:11; Joel 3:1

Psalm 85:2
[1]*Selah* may mean: *Pause, Crescendo* or *Musical interlude*
[a]Num 14:19; 1 Kin 8:34; Ps 78:38; 103:3; Jer 31:34
[b]Ps 32:1

Psalm 85:3
[a]Ps 78:38; 106:23
[b]Ex 32:12; Deut 13:17; Ps 106:23; Jon 3:9

Psalm 85:4
[a]Ps 80:3, 7
[b]Dan 9:16

Psalm 85:5
[1]Lit *generation and generation*
[a]Ps 74:1; 79:5; 80:4

Psalm 85:6
[1]Or *bring to life*
[a]Ps 71:20; 80:18
[b]Ps 33:1; 90:14; 149:2

Psalm 85:7
[a]Ps 106:4

Psalm 85:8
[1]Or *Let me hear*
[2]Lit *even to*
[3]Or *stupidity*
[a]Ps 29:11; Hag 2:9; Zech 9:10
[b]Ps 78:57; 2 Pet 2:21

Psalm 85:9
[1]Or *reverence*

[a]Ps 34:18; Is 46:13
[b]Ps 84:11; Hag 2:7; Zech 2:5; John 1:14

Psalm 85:10
[1]Or *faithfulness*
[a]Ps 25:10; 89:14; Prov 3:3
[b]Ps 72:3; Is 32:17

Psalm 85:11
[1]Or *Faithfulness*
[a]Is 45:8

Psalm 85:12
[a]Ps 84:11; James 1:17
[b]Lev 26:4; Ps 67:6; Ezek 34:27; Zech 8:12

Psalm 85:13
[a]Ps 89:14

Targum

Psa. 85:1 For praise; composed by the sons of Korah; a psalm. [2] You delighted, O LORD, in your land; you brought back the captivity of the house of Jacob. [3] You forgave the sins of your people; you covered all their faults forever. [4] You withdrew all your anger; you turned from the harshness of your anger. [5] Turn to us, O God our redemption; and revoke your anger against us. [6] Can it be that you will act harshly against us forever? Will you prolong out your harshness for all generations? [7] Will you not again revive us? And your people will rejoice in your word. [8] Show us, O LORD, your goodness; and may your redemption be given to us. [9] I will hear what God, the LORD, will say; for he will speak peace to his people and to his pious ones, and they will not return to heathenism. [10] Truly, his redemption is near to those who fear him, to make glory abide in our land. [11] Favor and truth meet, righteousness and peace have joined together. [12] Truth grew up from the land; and righteousness looked out from heaven. [13] Also the LORD will give what is good; and our land will give its produce. [14] Righteousness will walk before him; and he set his steps on a good path.

Spiritual Awareness

Introduction

This Psalm's subject is Israel's return from the Babylonian Exile to build the Second Temple. Unfortunately, the Second Temple was destroyed by the Romans in 70 CE. Israel has yearned for a permanent redemption in which the LORD will be wholly reconciled to His land. The fertility of the land was the most accurate measurement of the LORD's favorable attitude toward Israel. The LORD wants the earth to flourish, so His Chosen people will have a healthy and prosperous life.

Superscript

To the Sefirah Netzach who grants victory, by the sons of Korach, a psalm.

Verse two

You have forgiven the iniquity of Your people and covered up all their sins. Meditate on this verse.

Notes

The people in Exile pleaded to the LORD to allow them to return to their homeland. The land of Israel was promised to the Chosen People through the LORD's covenant with Abraham. While in Babylon, the people realized that their sins caused the LORD to respond harshly. The LORD sent prophets and messengers to the leaders of Judah. The message about their sins was clearly given. Yet the people continued to sin. The LORD had no choice but to bring the Babylonians to Judah to Exile the people. The worship of Tammuz and other gods in the Temple forced the Shekinah to leave the Temple. When this happened the Babylonians were able to destroy the Temple without any resistance. The Temple which was dedicated to the LORD was tainted with pagan worship. It was a sad day when the destruction of the Temple and Jerusalem.

Psalm 86

New American Standard 1995	Hebrew
Psa. 86:0 A Prayer of David. **Psa. 86:1** *ª*Incline Your ear, O LORD, *and* answer me; For I am *ᵇ*afflicted and needy. 2 *ª*Preserve my ¹soul, for I am a *ᵇ*godly man; O You my God, save Your servant who *ᶜ*trusts in You. 3 Be *ª*gracious to me, O Lord, For *ᵇ*to You I cry all day long. 4 Make glad the soul of Your servant, For to You, O Lord, *ª*I lift up my soul. 5 For You, Lord, are *ª*good, and *ᵇ*ready to forgive, And *ᶜ*abundant in lovingkindness to all who call upon You. 6 *ª*Give ear, O LORD, to my prayer; And give heed to the voice of my supplications! 7 In *ª*the day of my trouble I shall call upon You, For *ᵇ*You will answer me. 8 There is *ª*no one like You among the gods, O Lord, Nor are there any works *ᵇ*like Yours. 9 *ª*All nations whom You have made shall come and worship before You, O Lord, And they shall glorify Your name. 10 For You are *ª*great and *ᵇ*do ¹wondrous deeds;	תְּפִלָּה לְדָוִד הַטֵּה־יְהוָה **Psa. 86:1** ² אָזְנְךָ עֲנֵנִי כִּי־עָנִי וְאֶבְיוֹן אָנִי: שָׁמְרָה נַפְשִׁי כִּי־חָסִיד אָנִי הוֹשַׁע עַבְדְּךָ אַתָּה אֱלֹהַי הַבּוֹטֵחַ אֵלֶיךָ: ³ חָנֵּנִי אֲדֹנָי כִּי אֵלֶיךָ אֶקְרָא כָּל־ הַיּוֹם: ⁴ שַׂמֵּחַ נֶפֶשׁ עַבְדֶּךָ כִּי אֵלֶיךָ אֲדֹנָי נַפְשִׁי אֶשָּׂא: ⁵ כִּי־אַתָּה אֲדֹנָי טוֹב וְסַלָּח וְרַב־חֶסֶד לְכָל־ קֹרְאֶיךָ: ⁶ הַאֲזִינָה יְהוָה תְּפִלָּתִי וְהַקְשִׁיבָה בְּקוֹל תַּחֲנוּנוֹתָי: ⁷ בְּיוֹם צָרָתִי אֶקְרָאֶךָּ כִּי תַעֲנֵנִי: ⁸ אֵין־ כָּמוֹךָ בָאֱלֹהִים אֲדֹנָי וְאֵין כְּמַעֲשֶׂיךָ: ⁹ כָּל־גּוֹיִם אֲשֶׁר עָשִׂיתָ יָבוֹאוּ וְיִשְׁתַּחֲווּ לְפָנֶיךָ אֲדֹנָי וִיכַבְּדוּ לִשְׁמֶךָ: ¹⁰ כִּי־גָדוֹל אַתָּה וְעֹשֵׂה נִפְלָאוֹת אַתָּה אֱלֹהִים לְבַדֶּךָ: ¹¹ הוֹרֵנִי יְהוָה דַּרְכֶּךָ אֲהַלֵּךְ בַּאֲמִתֶּךָ יַחֵד לְבָבִי לְיִרְאָה שְׁמֶךָ: ¹² אוֹדְךָ אֲדֹנָי אֱלֹהַי בְּכָל־ לְבָבִי וַאֲכַבְּדָה שִׁמְךָ לְעוֹלָם: ¹³ כִּי־חַסְדְּךָ גָּדוֹל עָלָי וְהִצַּלְתָּ נַפְשִׁי מִשְּׁאוֹל תַּחְתִּיָּה: ¹⁴ אֱלֹהִים זֵדִים קָמוּ־עָלַי וַעֲדַת עָרִיצִים בִּקְשׁוּ נַפְשִׁי וְלֹא שָׂמוּךָ לְנֶגְדָּם: ¹⁵ וְאַתָּה

You alone *are God.

Psa. 86:11 *Teach me Your way, O LORD;

I will walk in Your truth;

*Unite my heart to fear Your name.

12 I will *give thanks to You, O Lord my God, with all my heart,

And will glorify Your name forever.

13 For Your lovingkindness toward me is great,

And You have *delivered my soul from the ¹depths of ²Sheol.

Psa. 86:14 O God, arrogant men have *risen up against me,

And ¹a band of violent men have sought my ²life,

And they have not set You before them.

15 But You, O Lord, are a God *merciful and gracious,

Slow to anger and abundant in lovingkindness and ¹truth.

16 *Turn to me, and be gracious to me;

Oh *grant Your strength to Your servant,

And save the *son of Your handmaid.

17 *Show me a sign for good,

That those who hate me may *see *it* and be ashamed,

Because You, O LORD, *have helped me and comforted me.

אֲדֹנָי אֵל־רַחוּם וְחַנּוּן אֶרֶךְ אַפַּיִם וְרַב־חֶסֶד וֶאֱמֶת: ¹⁶ פְּנֵה אֵלַי וְחָנֵּנִי תְּנָה־עֻזְּךָ לְעַבְדֶּךָ וְהוֹשִׁיעָה לְבֶן־אֲמָתֶךָ: ¹⁷ עֲשֵׂה־עִמִּי אוֹת לְטוֹבָה וְיִרְאוּ שֹׂנְאַי וְיֵבֹשׁוּ כִּי־אַתָּה יְהוָה עֲזַרְתַּנִי וְנִחַמְתָּנִי:

References

Psalm 86:1
*a*Ps 17:6; 31:2; 71:2
*b*Ps 40:17; 70:5

Psalm 86:2
[1]Or *life*
*a*Ps 25:20
*b*Ps 4:3; 50:5
*c*Ps 25:2; 31:14; 56:4

Psalm 86:3
*a*Ps 4:1; 57:1
*b*Ps 25:5; 88:9

Psalm 86:4
*a*Ps 25:1; 143:8

Psalm 86:5
*a*Ps 25:8
*b*Ps 130:4
*c*Ex 34:6; Neh 9:17; Ps 103:8; 145:8; Joel 2:13; Jon 4:2

Psalm 86:6
*a*Ps 55:1

Psalm 86:7
*a*Ps 50:15; 77:2
*b*Ps 17:6

Psalm 86:8
*a*Ex 15:11; 2 Sam 7:22; 1 Kin 8:23; Ps 89:6; Jer 10:6
*b*Deut 3:24

Psalm 86:9
*a*Ps 22:27; 66:4; Is 66:23; Rev 15:4

Psalm 86:10
[1]Or *miracles*

*a*Ps 77:13
*b*Ex 15:11; Ps 72:18; 77:14; 136:4
*c*Deut 6:4; 32:39; Ps 83:18; Is 37:16; 44:6, 8; Mark 12:29; 1 Cor 8:4

Psalm 86:11
*a*Ps 25:5
*b*Jer 32:39

Psalm 86:12
*a*Ps 111:1

Psalm 86:13
[1]Lit *lowest Sheol*
[2]I.e. the nether world
*a*Ps 30:3

Psalm 86:14
[1]Or *an assembly*
[2]Lit *soul*
*a*Ps 54:3

Psalm 86:15
[1]Or *faithfulness*
*a*Ps 86:5

Psalm 86:16
*a*Ps 25:16
*b*Ps 68:35
*c*Ps 116:16

Psalm 86:17
*a*Judg 6:17; Ps 119:122
*b*Ps 112:10
*c*Ps 118:13

Targum

Psa. 86:1 A prayer that David prayed. Incline, O LORD, your ear; answer me, for I am poor and needy. **²** Protect my soul, for I am pious; redeem your servant – you, O my God – for I do put my trust in you. **³** Have mercy on me, O LORD, for I will pray in your presence all the day. **⁴** Gladden the soul of your servant, for to you, O LORD, will I lift up my soul in prayer. **⁵** For you are the LORD, good to the righteous and forgiving to those who turn to his Torah, and multiplying favor to all who pray in your presence. **⁶** Hear, O LORD, my prayer; and accept the voice of my supplications. **⁷** On the day of my distress, I will call to you, for you answer me. **⁸** There is none besides you among the angels on high, O LORD, and there is nothing like your deeds. **⁹** All the Gentiles you have made shall come and bow down before you, O LORD; and they shall give glory to your name. **¹⁰** For you are great, O God, and you do wonders – you alone are God. **¹¹** Teach me, O LORD, your ways; I will walk in your truth; unify my heart to fear your name. **¹²** I will give thanks in your presence, O LORD my God, with all my heart; and I will glorify your name forever. **¹³** For your goodness towards me is great; and you have delivered my soul from lowest Sheol. **¹⁴** O God, arrogant men have risen against me, and mighty men have sought my soul; and they have not kept you in front of them. **¹⁵** And you, O LORD, are a God compassionate and merciful, putting away anger, and showing much favor and truth. **¹⁶** Turn unto me and pity me; give your strength to your servant, and redeem the son of your handmaiden. **¹⁷** Perform for me a miracle for good; when my son Solomon shall bring the ark into the sanctuary, let the gates be opened on my account and my enemies will see that you have forgiven me, and they will be ashamed and confess; for you are the LORD, you have helped me and comforted me.

Spiritual Awareness

Introduction

This Psalm describes the essential purpose of prayer. It is not a call for the LORD's assistance but the understanding that prayer makes your soul feel closer to the LORD.

Superscript and verse one

This is not a specific prayer of David. However, because of the accentuation, it is a general prayer of broad significance. All of the Psalms that pertain to a particular person's life should be viewed as being for the entire nation of Israel.

תְּפִלָּה (t'pheela) means "prayer." This word does not correspond to a "prayer," according to the sages. It is generally understood to be a plea or a request. It signifies an exercise for a person's inner self, which can be penetrated by acknowledging certain truths.

A prayer. By David. Incline Your ear, O LORD, answer me, for I am poor and defenseless.

Verse eight

The human soul needs to strive to be as near to the LORD as possible. This verse shows that pure monotheism had not been achieved by the surrounding nations and, to some degree, in Israel. She knew that there was one God who created Heaven and Earth. This was their God. However, at the point in history when this Psalm was written, the concept of one God was not quite in place yet.

There is none like You among the gods, O my Master, and none like Your creations.

Notes on this Psalm

The Psalmist cries out to the LORD and he/she strives to get closer spiritually. Verse eight also indicates that the Psalmist was concerned that his/her soul could be influenced by pagan gods. The Psalmist pleads with the LORD to help him/her to avoid that possibility. Even today people can be taken away from the LORD by the culture of society. People have different gods, like money, and power. When these gods convince a person to worship it then they give up their spiritual connection to the LORD. Hopefully, the person figures out when this happens and returns to the LORD.

52

Psalm 87

New American Standard 1995	Hebrew
Psa. 87:0 A Psalm of the sons of Korah. A Song. **Psa. 87:1** His *a*foundation is in the holy mountains. 2 The LORD *a*loves the gates of Zion More than all the *other* dwelling places of Jacob. 3 *a*Glorious things are spoken of you, O *b*city of God. [1]Selah. 4 "I shall mention [1a]Rahab and Babylon [2]among those who know Me; Behold, Philistia and *b*Tyre with [3c]Ethiopia: 'This one was born there.'" 5 But of Zion it shall be said, "This one and that one were born in her"; And the Most High Himself will *a*establish her. 6 The LORD will count when He *a*registers the peoples, "This one was born there." Selah. 7 Then those who *a*sing as well as those who [1b]play the flutes *shall say*, "All my *c*springs *of joy* are in you."	לִבְנֵי־קֹרַח מִזְמוֹר שִׁיר **Psa. 87:1** יְסוּדָתוֹ בְּהַרְרֵי־קֹדֶשׁ׃ 2 אֹהֵב יְהוָה 3 שַׁעֲרֵי צִיּוֹן מִכֹּל מִשְׁכְּנוֹת יַעֲקֹב׃ נִכְבָּדוֹת מְדֻבָּר בָּךְ עִיר הָאֱלֹהִים סֶלָה׃ 4 אַזְכִּיר רַהַב וּבָבֶל לְיֹדְעָי הִנֵּה פְלֶשֶׁת וְצוֹר עִם־כּוּשׁ זֶה יֻלַּד־ שָׁם׃ 5 וּלֲצִיּוֹן יֵאָמַר אִישׁ וְאִישׁ יֻלַּד־בָּהּ וְהוּא יְכוֹנְנֶהָ עֶלְיוֹן׃ 6 יְהוָה יִסְפֹּר בִּכְתוֹב עַמִּים זֶה יֻלַּד־ שָׁם סֶלָה׃ 7 וְשָׁרִים כְּחֹלְלִים כָּל־ מַעְיָנַי בָּךְ׃

References

Psalm 87:1
[a]Ps 78:69; Is 28:16

Psalm 87:2
[a]Ps 78:67, 68

Psalm 87:3
[1]*Selah* may mean: *Pause, Crescendo* or *Musical interlude*
[a]Is 60:1
[b]Ps 46:4; 48:8

Psalm 87:4
[1]I.e. Egypt
[2]Or *as*
[3]Lit *Cush*
[a]Job 9:13; Ps 89:10; Is 19:23-25
[b]Ps 45:12
[c]Ps 68:31

Psalm 87:5
[a]Ps 48:8

Psalm 87:6
[a]Ps 69:28; Is 4:3; Ezek 13:9

Psalm 87:7
[1]Or *dance*
[a]Ps 68:25; 149:3
[b]2 Sam 6:14; Ps 30:11
[c]Ps 36:9

Targum

Psa. 87:1 Uttered by the sons of Korah. A song that was established at the instruction of the fathers of old. [2] The LORD loves the entrances to the academies established in Zion more than all the synagogues of the house of Jacob. [3] Glorious words have been spoken of you, O city of God, forever. [4] The Egyptians and Babylonians have reminded those who know you of your praises; behold, the Philistines and Tyrians, with the Ethiopians; this king was brought up there. [5] And of Zion it will be said, "King David and Solomon his son were brought up within it; and God shall build it above." [6] O LORD, in the book in which they write the account of all the ages [it is written], "This king was brought up there forever." [7] And they utter songs with celebration – all kinds of psalms with sacrifice are uttered in your midst.

Spiritual Awareness

Introduction

Korach ran an unsuccessful revolt against Moses (Number 16). He felt he was superior to Moses, Aaron, and Israel's other leaders. He refused to recognize that the Land of Israel is holier than any other land in the world. Korach's sons refused to join their father in his revolt. Instead, they composed this Psalm to extol the unique virtues of the Land of Israel and the city of Jerusalem.

Verse three

They are honored through Him, Who is proclaimed within You, O city of God. Meditate on this verse.

Verse six

It was believed that the LORD had a book that listed people who had labored for the welfare of their own people. It was a short list for every nation.

The LORD counts when He registers peoples; This one was born there. Meditate on this verse.

Psalm 88

New American Standard 1995	Hebrew

Psa. 88:0 A Song. A Psalm of the sons of Korah. For the choir director; according to Mahalath Leannoth. A [†]Maskil of Heman [°]the Ezrahite.
 	
Psa. 88:1 O LORD, the [a]God of my salvation,
   I have [b]cried out by day and in the night before You.
2   Let my prayer [a]come before You;
   [b]Incline Your ear to my cry!
3   For my [a]soul has [1]had enough troubles,
   And [b]my life has drawn near to [2]Sheol.
4   I am reckoned among those who [a]go down to the pit;
   I have become like a man [b]without strength,
5   [1]Forsaken [a]among the dead,
   Like the slain who lie in the grave,
   Whom You remember no more,
   And they are [b]cut off from Your hand.
6   You have put me in [a]the lowest pit,
   In [b]dark places, in the [c]depths.
7   Your wrath [a]has rested upon me,
   And You have afflicted me with [b]all Your waves.   [1]Selah.
8   You have removed [a]my acquaintances far from me;
   You have made me an [1][b]object of loathing to them;
   I am [c]shut up and cannot go out.
	שִׁיר מִזְמוֹר לִבְנֵי קֹרַח **Psa. 88:1**
	לַמְנַצֵּחַ עַל־מָחֲלַת לְעַנּוֹת מַשְׂכִּיל
	לְהֵימָן הָאֶזְרָחִי ׃ ² יְהוָה אֱלֹהֵי
	יְשׁוּעָתִי יוֹם־צָעַקְתִּי בַלַּיְלָה נֶגְדֶּךָ ׃
	³ תָּבוֹא לְפָנֶיךָ תְּפִלָּתִי הַטֵּה־אָזְנְךָ
	לְרִנָּתִי ׃ ⁴ כִּי־שָׂבְעָה בְרָעוֹת נַפְשִׁי
	וְחַיַּי לִשְׁאוֹל הִגִּיעוּ ׃ ⁵ נֶחְשַׁבְתִּי
	עִם־יוֹרְדֵי בוֹר הָיִיתִי כְּגֶבֶר אֵין
	אֱיָל ׃ ⁶ בַּמֵּתִים חָפְשִׁי כְּמוֹ חֲלָלִים
	שֹׁכְבֵי קֶבֶר אֲשֶׁר לֹא זְכַרְתָּם עוֹד
	וְהֵמָּה מִיָּדְךָ נִגְזָרוּ ׃ ⁷ שַׁתַּנִי בְּבוֹר
	תַּחְתִּיּוֹת בְּמַחֲשַׁכִּים בִּמְצֹלוֹת ׃ ⁸
	עָלַי סָמְכָה חֲמָתֶךָ וְכָל־מִשְׁבָּרֶיךָ
	עִנִּיתָ סֶּלָה ׃ ⁹ הִרְחַקְתָּ מְיֻדָּעַי מִמֶּנִּי
	שַׁתַּנִי תוֹעֵבוֹת לָמוֹ כָּלֻא וְלֹא
	אֵצֵא ׃ ¹⁰ עֵינִי דָאֲבָה מִנִּי עֹנִי
	קְרָאתִיךָ יְהוָה בְּכָל־יוֹם שִׁטַּחְתִּי
	אֵלֶיךָ כַפָּי ׃ ¹¹ הֲלַמֵּתִים תַּעֲשֶׂה־
	פֶּלֶא אִם־רְפָאִים יָקוּמוּ ׀ יוֹדוּךָ
	סֶּלָה ׃ ¹² הַיְסֻפַּר בַּקֶּבֶר חַסְדֶּךָ
	אֱמוּנָתְךָ בָּאֲבַדּוֹן ׃ ¹³ הֲיִוָּדַע בַּחֹשֶׁךְ
	פִּלְאֶךָ וְצִדְקָתְךָ בְּאֶרֶץ נְשִׁיָּה ׃ ¹⁴
	וַאֲנִי ׀ אֵלֶיךָ יְהוָה שִׁוַּעְתִּי וּבַבֹּקֶר
	תְּפִלָּתִי תְקַדְּמֶךָּ ׃ ¹⁵ לָמָה יְהוָה

9 My [a]eye has wasted away because of affliction;

I have [b]called upon You every day, O LORD;

I have [c]spread out my [1]hands to You.

Psa. 88:10 Will You perform wonders for the dead?

Will [a]the [1]departed spirits rise *and* praise You? Selah.

11 Will Your lovingkindness be declared in the grave,

Your faithfulness in [1]Abaddon?

12 Will Your wonders be made known in the [a]darkness?

And Your [1]righteousness in the land of forgetfulness?

Psa. 88:13 But I, O LORD, have cried out [a]to You for help,

And [b]in the morning my prayer comes before You.

14 O LORD, why [a]do You reject my soul?

Why do You [b]hide Your face from me?

15 I was afflicted and [a]about to die from my youth on;

I suffer [b]Your terrors; I am [1]overcome.

16 Your [a]burning anger has passed over me;

Your terrors have [1b]destroyed me.

17 They have [a]surrounded me [b]like water all day long;

They have [c]encompassed me altogether.

18 You have removed [a]lover and friend far from me;

My acquaintances are *in* darkness.

תִּזְנַח נַפְשִׁי תַּסְתִּיר פָּנֶיךָ מִמֶּנִּי ׃ 16

עָנִי אֲנִי וְגֹוֵעַ מִנֹּעַר נָשָׂאתִי אֵמֶיךָ אָפוּנָה ׃ 17 עָלַי עָבְרוּ חֲרוֹנֶיךָ בִּעוּתֶיךָ צִמְּתוּתֻנִי ׃ 18 סַבּוּנִי כַמַּיִם כָּל־הַיֹּום הִקִּיפוּ עָלַי יָחַד ׃ 19 הִרְחַקְתָּ מִמֶּנִּי אֹהֵב וָרֵעַ מְיֻדָּעַי מַחְשָׁךְ ׃

References

Psalm 88:0
[†]Possibly, *Contemplative,* or *Didactic,* or *Skillful Psalm*
[°]1 Kin 4:31; 1 Chr 2:6; Ps 89: title

Psalm 88:1
[a]Ps 24:5; 27:9
[b]Ps 22:2; 86:3; Luke 18:7

Psalm 88:2
[a]Ps 18:6
[b]Ps 31:2; 86:1

Psalm 88:3
[1]Or *been satisfied with*
[2]I.e. the nether world
[a]Ps 107:26
[b]Ps 107:18; 116:3

Psalm 88:4
[a]Ps 28:1; 143:7
[b]Job 29:12; Ps 22:11

Psalm 88:5
[1]Lit *A freed one among the dead*
[a]Ps 31:12
[b]Ps 31:22; Is 53:8

Psalm 88:6
[a]Ps 86:13; Lam 3:55
[b]Ps 143:3
[c]Ps 69:15

Psalm 88:7
[1]*Selah* may mean: *Pause, Crescendo* or *Musical interlude*
[a]Ps 32:4; 39:10
[b]Ps 42:7

Psalm 88:8
[1]Lit *abomination to them*

[a]Job 19:13, 19; Ps 31:11; 142:4
[b]Job 30:10
[c]Ps 142:7; Jer 32:2; 36:5

Psalm 88:9
[1]Lit *palms*
[a]Ps 6:7; 31:9
[b]Ps 22:2; 86:3
[c]Job 11:13; Ps 143:6

Psalm 88:10
[1]Or *ghosts, shades*
[a]Ps 6:5; 30:9

Psalm 88:11
[1]I.e. place of destruction

Psalm 88:12
[1]I.e. faithfulness to His gracious promises
[a]Job 10:21; Ps 88:6

Psalm 88:13
[a]Ps 30:2
[b]Ps 5:3; 119:147

Psalm 88:14
[a]Ps 43:2; 44:9
[b]Job 13:24; Ps 13:1; 44:24

Psalm 88:15
[1]Or *embarrassed*
[a]Prov 24:11
[b]Job 6:4; 31:23

Psalm 88:16
[1]Or *silenced*
[a]2 Chr 28:11; Is 13:13; Lam 1:12
[b]Lam 3:54; Ezek 37:11

Psalm 88:17
[a]Ps 118:10-12

[b]Ps 124:4
[c]Ps 17:11; 22:12, 16

Psalm 88:18
[d]Job 19:13; Ps 88:8; 31:11; 38:11

Targum

Psa. 88:1 A song and a psalm composed by the sons of Korah, with a prayer; for praise; a good lesson composed by Heman the native. **2** O LORD God my redemption, daily I have made complaint; in the night my prayer is before you. **3** May my prayer come before you; incline your ear to my plea. [ANOTHER TARGUM: Let my prayer for your people, the house of Israel, come before you; and incline your ear to my psalm that I have sung for your glory.] **4** For my soul has had its fill of evils; and my life has arrived at Sheol. **5** I am reckoned with those who go down to the prison-house; I have become like a son of man who has no strength. **6** Like the wicked who died and did not return, having been made free from strife; like those slain by the sword, lying in the grave, whom you no longer remember, since they have been separated from the face of your presence. **7** You have placed me in exile, which is likened to the lower pit, among the oppressed in the depths. **8** Your fury rests on me, and all evil decrees have broken me; you have afflicted me forever. **9** You have removed those who know me far from me; you have made me loathsome to them; enclosed in prison, and I may not go out. **10** My eye has flowed with tears because of affliction; every day I have called to you, O LORD; I have spread my hands to you in prayer. **11** Could it be that you would work miracles for the dead? Or will bodies that have decayed in dust arise [and] give thanks in your presence forever? **12** Could it be that your goodness will be talked of in the grave? Your truth in the place of perdition? **13** Could it be that your wonders will be known in the darkness of Gehenna? And your generosity in the land of thirst and desolation? **14** But I have prayed in your presence, O LORD; and in the morning my prayer will come before you. **15** Why, O LORD, have you forsaken my soul, why will you hide your face from me, that I may not see illumination by your light? **16** I am afflicted and frail from childhood; I have borne the fear of you, loaded upon me. **17** Your anger has passed over me; your terrors have destroyed me. **18** They have surrounded me like water all day; they have encompassed me together. **19** You have removed friend and fellow far from me; as for those who know me, I am lowly in their mouth.

Spiritual Awareness

Introduction

It was believed by the people in exile that their situation was divinely ordained to spur Israel's spiritual development. The insecure Jews at that time had to learn to turn to the LORD for strength to find security and a purpose for their lives. The Psalmist adds that the Torah is home and that home is not a particular parcel of land. Another view is that people need to learn to place their lives in the hands of the LORD by living by the Torah. Materialism is not going to save the soul.

Superscript

Heiman was one of Korach's outstanding sons.

A psalm-song by the sons of Korach. To the Sefirah Netzach, who offers victory over a crushing pain, an instruction by Heiman the Ezrachi.

Verses 3 & 4

In exile, the people were beaten down because they could not worship the LORD as they did when the Temple stood in Jerusalem. They felt that their strength to continue was just about gone. They believed that they were disconnected from the LORD. Therefore, they cried out to the LORD to save them from the torture of separation.

For though my soul is sated with troubles, and my life has arrived at the grave.

If I am counted with them that are destined to go down into the grave if I have become as a man bereft of all strength,

Verse seven

Nevertheless Your wrath has clung fast to me, and You have taken the final strength from your billows. Meditate on this verse.

Verse ten

Do you work wonders for the dead, do the departed arise and render you homage? Meditate on this verse.

Notes on this Psalm

The Psalmist seems to be equating the troubles of Israel to that of a dead nation. The belief was that Sheol (Hell) was separate from the LORD. The LORD did not have jurisdiction in Sheol. Therefore, if one was sent to Sheol, that soul would be completely disconnected from the LORD. That was an unacceptable situation for the Hebrew people. The Exile in Babylon felt like being in Sheol.

Psalm 89

New American Standard 1995	Hebrew
Psa. 89:0 A †Maskil of °Ethan ˆthe Ezrahite. **Psa. 89:1** I will ᵃsing of the lovingkindness of the LORD forever; To all generations I will ᵇmake known Your ᶜfaithfulness with my mouth. 2 For I have said, "ᵃLovingkindness will be built up forever; In the heavens You will establish Your ᵇfaithfulness." 3 "I have made a covenant with ᵃMy chosen; I have ᵇsworn to David My servant, 4 I will establish your ᵃseed forever And build up your ᵇthrone to all generations."¹Selah. **Psa. 89:5** The ᵃheavens will praise Your wonders, O LORD; Your faithfulness also ᵇin the assembly of the ᶜholy ones. 6 For ᵃwho in the skies is comparable to the LORD? Who among the ¹ᵇsons of the mighty is like the LORD, 7 A God ᵃgreatly feared in the council of the ᵇholy ones, And ᶜawesome above all those who are around Him? 8 O LORD God of hosts, ᵃwho is like You, O mighty ¹LORD?	מַשְׂכִּיל לְאֵיתָן הָאֶזְרָחִי ׃ **Psa. 89:1** 2 חַסְדֵי יְהוָה עוֹלָם אָשִׁירָה לְדֹר וָדֹר ׀ אוֹדִיעַ אֱמוּנָתְךָ בְּפִי ׃ כִּי־ 3 אָמַרְתִּי עוֹלָם חֶסֶד יִבָּנֶה שָׁמַיִם ׀ תָּכִן אֱמוּנָתְךָ בָהֶם ׃ כָּרַתִּי בְרִית 4 לִבְחִירִי נִשְׁבַּעְתִּי לְדָוִד עַבְדִּי ׃ 5 עַד־עוֹלָם אָכִין זַרְעֶךָ וּבָנִיתִי לְדֹר־וָדוֹר כִּסְאֲךָ סֶלָה ׃ וְיוֹדוּ 6 שָׁמַיִם פִּלְאֲךָ יְהוָה אַף־אֱמוּנָתְךָ בִּקְהַל קְדֹשִׁים ׃ כִּי מִי בַשַּׁחַק 7 יַעֲרֹךְ לַיהוָה יִדְמֶה לַיהוָה בִּבְנֵי אֵלִים ׃ אֵל נַעֲרָץ בְּסוֹד־קְדֹשִׁים 8 רַבָּה וְנוֹרָא עַל־כָּל־סְבִיבָיו ׃ 9 יְהוָה ׀ אֱלֹהֵי צְבָאוֹת מִי־כָמוֹךָ חֲסִין ׀ יָהּ וֶאֱמוּנָתְךָ סְבִיבוֹתֶיךָ ׃ 10 אַתָּה מוֹשֵׁל בְּגֵאוּת הַיָּם בְּשׂוֹא גַלָּיו אַתָּה תְשַׁבְּחֵם ׃ אַתָּה דִכִּאתָ 11 כֶחָלָל רָהַב בִּזְרוֹעַ עֻזְּךָ פִּזַּרְתָּ אוֹיְבֶיךָ ׃ לְךָ שָׁמַיִם אַף־לְךָ אָרֶץ 12 תֵּבֵל וּמְלֹאָהּ אַתָּה יְסַדְתָּם ׃ צָפוֹן 13 וְיָמִין אַתָּה בְרָאתָם תָּבוֹר וְחֶרְמוֹן בְּשִׁמְךָ יְרַנֵּנוּ ׃ לְךָ זְרוֹעַ עִם־ 14 גְּבוּרָה תָּעֹז יָדְךָ תָּרוּם יְמִינֶךָ ׃ 15 צֶדֶק וּמִשְׁפָּט מְכוֹן כִּסְאֶךָ חֶסֶד

<table>
<tr><td>

Your faithfulness also surrounds You.

9 You rule the swelling of the sea;
When its waves rise, You [a]still them.

10 You Yourself crushed [1a]Rahab like one who is slain;
You [b]scattered Your enemies with [2]Your mighty arm.

Psa. 89:11 The [a]heavens are Yours, the earth also is Yours;
The [b]world and [1]all it contains, You have founded them.

12 The [a]north and the south, You have created them;
[b]Tabor and [c]Hermon [d]shout for joy at Your name.

13 You have [1]a strong arm;
Your hand is mighty, Your [a]right hand is exalted.

14 [a]Righteousness and justice are the foundation of Your throne;
[b]Lovingkindness and [1]truth go before You.

15 How blessed are the people who know the [1a]joyful sound!
O LORD, they walk in the [b]light of Your countenance.

16 In [a]Your name they rejoice all the day,
And by Your righteousness they are exalted.

17 For You are the glory of [a]their strength,
And by Your favor [1]our [b]horn is exalted.

18 For our [a]shield belongs to the LORD,
[1]And our king to the [b]Holy One of Israel.

</td><td dir="rtl">

וֶאֱמֶת יְקַדְּמוּ פָנֶיךָ ׃ 16 אַשְׁרֵי הָעָם
יוֹדְעֵי תְרוּעָה יְהוָֹה בְּאוֹר־פָּנֶיךָ
יְהַלֵּכוּן ׃ 17 בְּשִׁמְךָ יְגִילוּן כָּל־הַיּוֹם
וּבְצִדְקָתְךָ יָרוּמוּ ׃ 18 כִּי־תִפְאֶרֶת
עֻזָּמוֹ אָתָּה וּבִרְצֹנְךָ תָּרִים [תָּרוּם]
קַרְנֵנוּ ׃ 19 כִּי לַיהוָה מָגִנֵּנוּ וְלִקְדוֹשׁ
יִשְׂרָאֵל מַלְכֵּנוּ ׃ 20 אָז דִּבַּרְתָּ בְחָזוֹן
לַחֲסִידֶיךָ וַתֹּאמֶר שִׁוִּיתִי עֵזֶר עַל־
גִּבּוֹר הֲרִימוֹתִי בָחוּר מֵעָם ׃ 21
מָצָאתִי דָּוִד עַבְדִּי בְּשֶׁמֶן קָדְשִׁי
מְשַׁחְתִּיו ׃ 22 אֲשֶׁר יָדִי תִּכּוֹן עִמּוֹ
אַף־זְרוֹעִי תְאַמְּצֶנּוּ ׃ 23 לֹא־יַשִּׁא
אוֹיֵב בּוֹ וּבֶן־עַוְלָה לֹא יְעַנֶּנּוּ ׃ 24
וְכַתּוֹתִי מִפָּנָיו צָרָיו וּמְשַׂנְאָיו
אֶגּוֹף ׃ 25 וֶאֱמוּנָתִי וְחַסְדִּי עִמּוֹ
וּבִשְׁמִי תָּרוּם קַרְנוֹ ׃ 26 וְשַׂמְתִּי בַיָּם
יָדוֹ וּבַנְּהָרוֹת יְמִינוֹ ׃ 27 הוּא יִקְרָאֵנִי
אָבִי אָתָּה אֵלִי וְצוּר יְשׁוּעָתִי ׃ 28
אַף־אָנִי בְּכוֹר אֶתְּנֵהוּ עֶלְיוֹן
לְמַלְכֵי־אָרֶץ ׃ 29 לְעוֹלָם אֶשְׁמוֹר־
[אֶשְׁמָר]־לוֹ חַסְדִּי וּבְרִיתִי נֶאֱמֶנֶת
לוֹ ׃ 30 וְשַׂמְתִּי לָעַד זַרְעוֹ וְכִסְאוֹ
כִּימֵי שָׁמָיִם ׃ 31 אִם־יַעַזְבוּ בָנָיו
תּוֹרָתִי וּבְמִשְׁפָּטַי לֹא יֵלֵכוּן ׃ 32
אִם־חֻקֹּתַי יְחַלֵּלוּ וּמִצְוֹתַי לֹא
יִשְׁמֹרוּ ׃ 33 וּפָקַדְתִּי בְשֵׁבֶט פִּשְׁעָם
וּבִנְגָעִים עֲוֹנָם ׃ 34 וְחַסְדִּי לֹא־אָפִיר
מֵעִמּוֹ וְלֹא־אֲשַׁקֵּר בֶּאֱמוּנָתִי ׃ 35

</td></tr>
</table>

Psa. 89:19   [1]Once You spoke in vision to Your godly [2]ones,

    And said, "I have [3]given help to one who is [a]mighty;

    I have exalted one [b]chosen from the people.

[20]   "I have [a]found David My servant;

    With My holy [b]oil I have anointed him,

[21]   With whom [a]My hand will be established;

    My arm also will [b]strengthen him.

[22]   "The enemy will not [1]deceive him,

    Nor the [2a]son of wickedness afflict him.

[23]   "But I shall [a]crush his adversaries before him,

    And strike those who hate him.

[24]   "My [a]faithfulness and My lovingkindness will be with him,

    And in My name his [b]horn will be exalted.

[25]   "I shall also set his hand [a]on the sea

    And his right hand on the rivers.

[26]   "He will cry to Me, 'You are [a]my Father,

    My God, and the [b]rock of my salvation.'

[27]   "I also shall make him *My* [a]firstborn,

    The [b]highest of the kings of the earth.

[28]   "My [a]lovingkindness I will keep for him forever,

    And My [b]covenant shall be confirmed to him.

[29]   "So I will establish his [1a]descendants forever

לֹא־אֲחַלֵּל בְּרִיתִי וּמוֹצָא שְׂפָתַי לֹא אֲשַׁנֶּה׃ 36 אַחַת נִשְׁבַּעְתִּי בְקָדְשִׁי אִם־לְדָוִד אֲכַזֵּב׃ 37 זַרְעוֹ לְעוֹלָם יִהְיֶה וְכִסְאוֹ כַשֶּׁמֶשׁ נֶגְדִּי׃ 38 כְּיָרֵחַ יִכּוֹן עוֹלָם וְעֵד בַּשַּׁחַק נֶאֱמָן סֶלָה׃ 39 וְאַתָּה זָנַחְתָּ וַתִּמְאָס הִתְעַבַּרְתָּ עִם־מְשִׁיחֶךָ׃ 40 נֵאַרְתָּה בְּרִית עַבְדֶּךָ חִלַּלְתָּ לָאָרֶץ נִזְרוֹ׃ 41 פָּרַצְתָּ כָל־גְּדֵרֹתָיו שַׂמְתָּ מִבְצָרָיו מְחִתָּה׃ 42 שַׁסֻּהוּ כָּל־עֹבְרֵי דָרֶךְ הָיָה חֶרְפָּה לִשְׁכֵנָיו׃ 43 הֲרִימוֹתָ יְמִין צָרָיו הִשְׂמַחְתָּ כָּל־אוֹיְבָיו׃ 44 אַף־תָּשִׁיב צוּר חַרְבּוֹ וְלֹא הֲקֵימֹתוֹ בַּמִּלְחָמָה׃ 45 הִשְׁבַּתָּ מִטְּהָרוֹ וְכִסְאוֹ לָאָרֶץ מִגַּרְתָּה׃ 46 הִקְצַרְתָּ יְמֵי עֲלוּמָיו הֶעֱטִיתָ עָלָיו בּוּשָׁה סֶלָה׃ 47 עַד־מָה יְהוָה תִּסָּתֵר לָנֶצַח תִּבְעַר כְּמוֹ־אֵשׁ חֲמָתֶךָ׃ 48 זְכָר־אֲנִי מֶה־חָלֶד עַל־מַה־שָּׁוְא בָּרָאתָ כָל־בְּנֵי־אָדָם׃ 49 מִי גֶבֶר יִחְיֶה וְלֹא יִרְאֶה־מָּוֶת יְמַלֵּט נַפְשׁוֹ מִיַּד־שְׁאוֹל סֶלָה׃ 50 אַיֵּה חֲסָדֶיךָ הָרִאשֹׁנִים אֲדֹנָי נִשְׁבַּעְתָּ לְדָוִד בֶּאֱמוּנָתֶךָ׃ 51 זְכֹר אֲדֹנָי חֶרְפַּת עֲבָדֶיךָ שְׂאֵתִי בְחֵיקִי כָּל־רַבִּים עַמִּים׃ 52 אֲשֶׁר חֵרְפוּ אוֹיְבֶיךָ יְהוָה אֲשֶׁר חֵרְפוּ עִקְּבוֹת מְשִׁיחֶךָ׃ 53 בָּרוּךְ יְהוָה לְעוֹלָם אָמֵן וְאָמֵן׃

And his [b]throne [c]as the days of heaven.

Psa. 89:30　　　　"If his sons [a]forsake My law
　　　And do not walk in My judgments,
31　　　If they [1]violate My statutes
　　　And do not keep My commandments,
32　　　Then I will punish their transgression with the [a]rod
　　　And their iniquity with stripes.
33　　　"But I will not break off [a]My lovingkindness from him,
　　　Nor deal falsely in My faithfulness.
34　　　"My [a]covenant I will not [1]violate,
　　　Nor will I [b]alter [2]the utterance of My lips.
35　　　"[1]Once I have [a]sworn by My holiness;
　　　I will not lie to David.
36　　　"His [1a]descendants shall endure forever
　　　And his [b]throne [c]as the sun before Me.
37　　　"It shall be established forever [a]like the moon,
　　　And the [b]witness in the sky is faithful."　　[1]Selah.

Psa. 89:38　　　　But You have [a]cast off and [b]rejected,
　　　You have been full of wrath [1]against Your [c]anointed.
39　　　You have [a]spurned the covenant of Your servant;
　　　You have [b]profaned [c]his crown [1]in the dust.

40 You have *a*broken down all his walls;

You have *b*brought his strongholds to ruin.

41 *a*All who pass along the way plunder him;

He has become a *b*reproach to his neighbors.

42 You have *a*exalted the right hand of his adversaries;

You have *b*made all his enemies rejoice.

43 You also turn back the edge of his sword

And have *a*not made him stand in battle.

44 You have made his [1]*a*splendor to cease

And cast his throne to the ground.

45 You have *a*shortened the days of his youth;

You have *b*covered him with shame. Selah.

Psa. 89:46 *a*How long, O LORD?

Will You hide Yourself forever?
Will Your *b*wrath burn like fire?

47 *a*Remember [1]what my span of life is;

For what *b*vanity [2]You have created all the sons of men!

48 What man can live and not *a*see death?

Can he *b*deliver his soul from the [1]power of [2]Sheol? Selah.

Psa. 89:49 Where are Your former lovingkindnesses, O Lord,

<table>
<tr><td>

Which You [a]swore to David in Your faithfulness?

50 Remember, O Lord, the [a]reproach of Your servants;

[1]How I bear in my bosom *the reproach of* all the many peoples,

51 With which [a]Your enemies have reproached, O LORD,

With which they have reproached the footsteps of [b]Your anointed.

Psa. 89:52 [a]Blessed be the LORD forever!

Amen and Amen.

</td><td></td></tr>
</table>

References

Psalm 89:0
[a]Ps 59:16; 101:1
[b]Ps 40:10
[c]Ps 36:5; 88:11; 89:5, 8, 24, 33, 49; 92:2; 119:90; Is 25:1; Lam 3:23

Psalm 89:2
[a]Ps 103:17
[b]Ps 36:5; 119:90

Psalm 89:3
[a]1 Kin 8:16
[b]Ps 132:11

Psalm 89:4
[1]*Selah* may mean: *Pause, Crescendo* or *Musical interlude*
[a]2 Sam 7:16
[b]2 Sam 7:13; Is 9:7; Luke 1:33

Psalm 89:5
[a]Ps 19:1; 97:6
[b]Ps 149:1
[c]Job 5:1

Psalm 89:6
[1]Or *sons of gods*
[a]Ps 86:8; 113:5
[b]Ps 29:1; 82:1

Psalm 89:7
[a]Ps 47:2; 68:35; 76:7, 11
[b]Ps 89:5
[c]Ps 96:4

Psalm 89:8
[1]Heb *YAH*
[a]Ps 35:10; 71:19

Psalm 89:9

[a]Ps 65:7; 107:29

Psalm 89:10
[1]I.e. Egypt
[2]Lit *the arm of Your might*
[a]Ps 87:4; Is 30:7; 51:9
[b]Ps 18:14; 68:1; 144:6

Psalm 89:11
[1]Lit *its fullness*
[a]Gen 1:1; 1 Chr 29:11; Ps 96:5
[b]Ps 24:1

Psalm 89:12
[a]Job 26:7
[b]Josh 19:22; Judg 4:6; Jer 46:18
[c]Deut 3:8; Josh 11:17; 12:1; Ps 133:3; Song 4:8
[d]Ps 98:8

Psalm 89:13
[1]Lit *an arm with strength*
[a]Ps 98:1; 118:16

Psalm 89:14
[1]Or *faithfulness*
[a]Ps 97:2
[b]Ps 85:13

Psalm 89:15
[1]Or *blast of the trumpet, shout of joy*
[a]Lev 23:24; Num 10:10; Ps 98:6
[b]Ps 4:6; 44:3; 67:1; 80:3; 90:8

Psalm 89:16
[a]Ps 105:3

Psalm 89:17
[1]Another reading is *You exalt our horn*
[a]Ps 28:8
[b]Ps 75:10; 92:10; 148:14

Psalm 89:18
[1]Or *Even to the Holy One of Israel our King*
[a]Ps 47:9
[b]Ps 71:22; 78:41

Psalm 89:19
[1]Or *At that time*
[2]Some mss read *one*
[3]Lit *placed help upon*
[a]2 Sam 17:10
[b]1 Kin 11:34; Ps 78:70

Psalm 89:20
[a]1 Sam 13:14; 16:1-12; Acts 13:22
[b]1 Sam 16:13

Psalm 89:21
[a]Ps 18:35; 80:17
[b]Ps 18:32

Psalm 89:22
[1]Or *exact usury from him*
[2]Or *wicked man*
[a]2 Sam 7:10; Ps 125:3

Psalm 89:23
[a]2 Sam 7:9; Ps 18:40

Psalm 89:24
[a]Ps 89:1
[b]Ps 132:17

Psalm 89:25
[a]Ps 72:8

Psalm 89:26
[a]2 Sam 7:14; 1 Chr 22:10; Jer 3:19
[b]2 Sam 22:47; Ps 95:1

Psalm 89:27
[a]Ex 4:22; Ps 2:7; Jer 31:9; Col 1:15, 18

[b]Num 24:7; Ps 72:11; Rev 19:16

Psalm 89:28
[a]Ps 89:33
[b]Ps 89:3, 34

Psalm 89:29
[1]Lit *seed*
[a]Ps 18:50; 89:4, 36
[b]1 Kin 2:4; Ps 89:4; 132:12; Is 9:7; Jer 33:17
[c]Deut 11:21

Psalm 89:30
[a]2 Sam 7:14; Ps 119:53

Psalm 89:31
[1]Lit *profane*

Psalm 89:32
[a]Job 9:34; 21:9

Psalm 89:33
[a]2 Sam 7:15

Psalm 89:34
[1]Lit *profane*
[2]Lit *that which goes forth*
[a]Deut 7:9; Jer 33:20, 21
[b]Num 23:19

Psalm 89:35
[1]Or *One thing*
[a]Ps 60:6; Amos 4:2

Psalm 89:36
[1]Lit *seed*
[a]Ps 89:29; Luke 1:33
[b]Ps 72:5
[c]Ps 72:17

Psalm 89:37

[1]*Selah* may mean: *Pause, Crescendo* or *Musical interlude*
[a]Ps 72:5
[b]Job 16:19

Psalm 89:38
[1]Lit *with*
[a]Ps 44:9
[b]Deut 32:19; 1 Chr 28:9
[c]Ps 20:6; 89:20, 51

Psalm 89:39
[1]Lit *to the ground*
[a]Ps 78:59; Lam 2:7
[b]Ps 74:7
[c]Lam 5:16

Psalm 89:40
[a]Ps 80:12
[b]Lam 2:2, 5

Psalm 89:41
[a]Ps 80:12
[b]Ps 44:13; 69:9, 19; 79:4

Psalm 89:42
[a]Ps 13:2
[b]Ps 80:6

Psalm 89:43
[a]Ps 44:10

Psalm 89:44
[1]Lit *clearness, luster*
[a]Ezek 28:7

Psalm 89:45
[a]Ps 102:23
[b]Ps 44:15; 71:13; 109:29

Psalm 89:46
[a]Ps 13:1; 44:24

[b]Ps 79:5; 80:4

Psalm 89:47
[1]Lit *of what duration I am*
[2]Or *have You...men?*
[a]Job 7:7; 10:9; 14:1
[b]Ps 39:5; 62:9; Eccl 1:2; 2:11

Psalm 89:48
[1]Lit *hand*
[2]I.e. the nether world
[a]Ps 22:29; 49:9
[b]Ps 49:15

Psalm 89:49
[a]2 Sam 7:15; Jer 30:9; Ezek 34:23

Psalm 89:50
[1]Lit *My bearing in my bosom*
[a]Ps 69:9; 74:18, 22

Psalm 89:51
[a]Ps 74:10, 18, 22
[b]Ps 89:38

Psalm 89:52
[a]Ps 41:13; 72:19; 106:48

Targum

Psa. 89:1 A good lesson uttered by Abraham, who came from the east. [2] I will praise the kindness of the LORD forever; from generation to generation I will make known your truth with my mouth. [3] For I said, "The world will be built by kindness; you will establish your truth in the heavens." [4] I made a covenant with Abraham my chosen; I confirmed it with my servant David. [5] I will establish your sons forever; and for every generation I will build your royal throne forever. [6] And the heavens will confess your wonders, O LORD; also your truth in the assembly of the holy ones. [7] For who in the clouds can be set beside the LORD? Who resembles the LORD in the multitudes of angels? [8] God is mighty in the mysteries of the holy ones; sitting on the throne of glory, great and fearsome over all the angels who stand around him. [9] O LORD God above the hosts of the height, who is like you in strength, O LORD? And your truth is around you. [10] You rule over the pride of the sea; when its waves increase and become high, you will subdue them. [11] You have crushed Rahab, that is, wicked Pharaoh, like one slain by the sword; with the might of your strong arm you have scattered your enemies. [12] Yours is the heaven, yea, yours is the earth; you have founded the world and all its contents. [13] The deserts in the north and those who dwell in the south, you created them; Tabor in the west and Hermon in the east sing praise in your name. [14] Yours is the arm with strength; your hand will be strong to redeem your people; your right hand will be raised to perfect your sanctuary. [15] Righteousness and justice are the dwelling place of your glorious throne; favor and truth go before your face. [16] Happy the people who know to please their creator with a shout; O LORD, in the splendid light of your countenance they will walk and be acquitted in judgment. [17] In your name they will rejoice all day, and by your righteousness they will be exalted. [18] For you are the splendor of their strength, and by your will their horn is exalted. [19] For our shields belong to the LORD, and our king belongs to the LORD, the Holy One of Israel. [20] Then you spoke in a vision to your pious ones, and you said, "I have set up a helper for my people by the hand of one mighty in Torah; I have set apart a youth from among the people." [21] I have found David my servant, with the holy oil I anointed him. [22] Whom my hands are ready to help; truly my arm will strengthen him. [23] The enemy will not make him go astray; the son of wickedness will not afflict him. [24] And I will crush his oppressors before him, and I will smite his foes. [25] And my truth and goodness are with him; in the name of my word his glory will be exalted. [26] And I will place his dominion at the harbors of the sea, and the might of his right hand on those who dwell by the rivers. [27] He will call to me, "You are my father (abba), my God, and the strength of my redemption." [28] Also I will make him first-born of the kings of the house of Judah, the highest of the kings of the earth. [29] I will preserve my goodness to him forever; and my covenant is constant for him. [30] And I will set up his sons forever, and his throne for as many days as the heavens will last. [31] If his sons abandon my Torah, and do not walk in my judgments, [32] If they violate my covenant, and do not keep my commandments, [33]

Then I will punish their rebellions by means of the rod of the wicked, and their iniquities by the demons that plague them. [34] But my goodness I will not revoke from him, and I will not be false to my faithfulness. [35] I will not violate my covenant, and the utterance of my lips I will not change. [36] Once I have sworn by my holy name: "I will not lie to David." [37] His sons will exist forever, and his throne is bright as the sun before me. [38] Like the moon that is set for an eternal sign, and a faithful witness in the sky forever. [39] But you have forsaken and rejected, grown angry with your anointed. [40] You have changed the covenant with your servant; you have profaned his crown to the earth. [41] You have forced all his strongholds, you have made his open villages a ruin. [42] All who pass on the road have trampled him; he has become a disgrace to his neighbors. [43] You have raised the right hand of his oppressors; you have gladdened all his enemies. [44] Also you will turn aside his sword and you have not supported him in battle. [45] You have abolished the priests who sprinkle [blood] on the altar and cleanse his people, and you have cast to the ground his royal throne. [46] You have cut short the days of his young men; you have covered him with shame and disgrace forever. [47] How long, O LORD, will you remove your presence forever? [How long] will your rage burn like fire? [48] Remember that I was created from dust; why have you created all the sons of men for vanity? [49] Who is the man who will live and not see the angel of death, who will deliver his soul from his hand, and not go down to his grave forever? [50] Where are your favors which were from the beginning, O LORD, which you swore to David in your faithfulness? [51] Remember, O LORD, the disgrace of your servant; I have borne in my bosom all the insults of many peoples. [52] For your enemies have scorned, O LORD, for they have scorned the delay of the footsteps of your Messiah, O LORD. [53] Blessed be the name of the LORD in this age, amen and amen. Blessed be the name of the LORD in the age to come, amen and amen. --

Spiritual Awareness

Introduction

This Psalm records the agreement that the LORD struck with King David. The LORD promised that if David and his offspring remained faithful to Him, He would be true to them. However, exile and suffering would occur if the offspring betrayed the covenant.

Superscript

"Ethan the Ezrahite is the songwriter-author of Psalm 89. The title of that Psalm says it is "a maskil of Ethan the Ezrahite." In addition to Psalm 89, Ethan the Ezrahite is mentioned in 1 Kings 4:31 as a wise man, yet not as wise as King Solomon, who "was wiser than anyone else, including Ethan the Ezrahite." First Chronicles 2:6 gives the added information that Ethan had four brothers and was the son of Zerah (called Mahol in 1 Kings 4:31). He was of the tribe of Levi.

First Chronicles 15:17 mentions an Ethan who was involved with bringing of the Ark of the Covenant to Jerusalem. Since he is called "Ethan the son of Kushaiah," he is probably a different person from the author of Psalm 89. However, 1 Chronicles 15:19 adds that the son of Kushaiah was a musician, one of the men to sound the bronze cymbals, and this had led some scholars to assume a link between the two Ethans. If they are the same person, then Ethan the Ezrahite is probably also known as Jeduthun (1 Chronicles 16:38–42 and the titles of Psalms 62 and 77)."[2]

---

[2] GotQuestions.org, "Home," GotQuestions.org, March 23, 2015, https://www.gotquestions.org/Ethan-the-Ezrahite.html.

Verse four

I shall prepare your descendants forever and shall build up your throne for generations upon generations. Meditate on this verse.

Verse thirty-seven

As the moon shall be established forever, he shall remain a faithful witness in the sky. Meditate on this verse.

Verse forty-six

You have caused the days of his youth to be short and have spread shame over him. Meditate on this verse.

Verse forty-eight

Where is there a man who truly lives and shall not see death, who knows how to deliver his soul from the power of the grave? Meditate on this verse.

Psalm 90

New American Standard 1995	Hebrew

Psa. 90:0   A Prayer of [†]Moses, the man of God.

Psa. 90:1   Lord, You have been our [1a]dwelling place in all generations.

2   Before [a]the mountains were born [1]Or You [b]gave birth to the earth and the world,

Even [c]from everlasting to everlasting, You are God.

Psa. 90:3   You [a]turn man back into dust

And say, "Return, O children of men."

4   For [a]a thousand years in Your sight

Are like [b]yesterday when it passes by,

[1]Or *as* a [c]watch in the night.

5   You [a]have [1]swept them away like a flood, they [2b]fall asleep;

In the morning they are like [c]grass which [3]sprouts anew.

6   In the morning it [a]flourishes and [1]sprouts anew;

Toward evening it [b]fades and [c]withers away.

Psa. 90:7   For we have been [a]consumed by Your anger

And by Your wrath we have been [1]dismayed.

תְּפִלָּה לְמֹשֶׁה אִישׁ־ **Psa. 90:1**
הָאֱלֹהִים אֲדֹנָי מָעוֹן אַתָּה הָיִיתָ
לָּנוּ בְּדֹר וָדֹר ׃ 2 בְּטֶרֶם ׀ הָרִים
יֻלָּדוּ וַתְּחוֹלֵל אֶרֶץ וְתֵבֵל וּמֵעוֹלָם
עַד־עוֹלָם אַתָּה אֵל ׃ 3 תָּשֵׁב אֱנוֹשׁ
עַד־דַּכָּא וַתֹּאמֶר שׁוּבוּ בְנֵי־אָדָם ׃
4 כִּי אֶלֶף שָׁנִים בְּעֵינֶיךָ כְּיוֹם
אֶתְמוֹל כִּי יַעֲבֹר וְאַשְׁמוּרָה
בַלָּיְלָה ׃ 5 זְרַמְתָּם שֵׁנָה יִהְיוּ בַּבֹּקֶר
כֶּחָצִיר יַחֲלֹף ׃ 6 בַּבֹּקֶר יָצִיץ וְחָלָף
לָעֶרֶב יְמוֹלֵל וְיָבֵשׁ ׃ 7 כִּי־כָלִינוּ
בְאַפֶּךָ וּבַחֲמָתְךָ נִבְהָלְנוּ ׃ 8 שַׁתָּ
[שַׁתָּה] עֲוֺנֹתֵינוּ לְנֶגְדֶּךָ עֲלֻמֵנוּ
לִמְאוֹר פָּנֶיךָ ׃ 9 כִּי כָל־יָמֵינוּ פָּנוּ
בְעֶבְרָתֶךָ כִּלִּינוּ שָׁנֵינוּ כְמוֹ־הֶגֶה ׃
10 יְמֵי־שְׁנוֹתֵינוּ בָהֶם שִׁבְעִים שָׁנָה
וְאִם בִּגְבוּרֹת ׀ שְׁמוֹנִים שָׁנָה
וְרָהְבָּם עָמָל וָאָוֶן כִּי־גָז חִישׁ
וַנָּעֻפָה ׃ 11 מִי־יוֹדֵעַ עֹז אַפֶּךָ
וּכְיִרְאָתְךָ עֶבְרָתֶךָ ׃ 12 לִמְנוֹת יָמֵינוּ
כֵּן הוֹדַע וְנָבִא לְבַב חָכְמָה ׃ 13
שׁוּבָה יְהוָה עַד־מָתָי וְהִנָּחֵם עַל־
עֲבָדֶיךָ ׃ 14 שַׂבְּעֵנוּ בַבֹּקֶר חַסְדֶּךָ

8 You have [a]placed our iniquities before You,

Our [b]secret *sins* in the light of Your presence.

9 For [a]all our days have declined in Your fury;

We have finished our years like a [1]sigh.

10 As for the days of our [1]life, [2]they contain seventy years,

Or if due to strength, [a]eighty years,

Yet their pride is *but* [b]labor and sorrow;

For soon it is gone and we [c]fly away.

11 Who [1]understands the [a]power of Your anger

And Your fury, according to the [b]fear [2]that is due You?

12 So [a]teach us to number our days,

That we may [1b]present to You a heart of wisdom.

Psa. 90:13 Do [a]return, O LORD; [b]how long *will it be?*

And [1]be [c]sorry for Your servants.

14 O [a]satisfy us in the morning with Your lovingkindness,

That we may [b]sing for joy and be glad all our days.

15 [a]Make us glad [1]according to the days You have afflicted us,

And the [b]years we have seen [2]evil.

16 Let Your [a]work appear to Your servants

And Your [b]majesty [1]to their children.

17 Let the [a]favor of the Lord our God be upon us;

וּנְרַנְּנָה וְנִשְׂמְחָה בְּכָל־יָמֵינוּ : 15

שַׂמְּחֵנוּ כִּימוֹת עִנִּיתָנוּ שְׁנוֹת רָאִינוּ

רָעָה : 16 יֵרָאֶה אֶל־עֲבָדֶיךָ פָעֳלֶךָ

וַהֲדָרְךָ עַל־בְּנֵיהֶם : 17 וִיהִי ׀ נֹעַם

אֲדֹנָי אֱלֹהֵינוּ עָלֵינוּ וּמַעֲשֵׂה יָדֵינוּ

כּוֹנְנָה עָלֵינוּ וּמַעֲשֵׂה יָדֵינוּ

כּוֹנְנֵהוּ :

And [1b]confirm for us the work of our hands; Yes, [1]confirm the work of our hands.	

References

Psalm 90:0
[†]Deut 33:1

Psalm 90:1
[1]Or *hiding place;* some ancient mss read *place of refuge*
[a]Deut 33:27; Ps 71:3; 91:1; Ezek 11:16

Psalm 90:2
[1]Or *And*
[a]Job 15:7; Prov 8:25
[b]Gen 1:1; Ps 102:25; 104:5
[c]Ps 93:2; 102:24, 27; Jer 10:10

Psalm 90:3
[a]Gen 3:19; Job 34:14, 15; Ps 104:29

Psalm 90:4
[1]Or *And*
[a]2 Pet 3:8
[b]Ps 39:5
[c]Ex 14:24; Judg 7:19

Psalm 90:5
[1]Or *flooded*
[2]Lit *become asleep*
[3]Or *passes away*
[a]Job 22:16; 27:20
[b]Job 14:12; 20:8; Ps 76:5
[c]Ps 103:15; Is 40:6

Psalm 90:6
[1]Or *passes away*
[a]Job 14:2
[b]Ps 92:7; Matt 6:30
[c]James 1:11

Psalm 90:7

[1]Or *terrified*
[a]Ps 39:11

Psalm 90:8
[a]Ps 50:21; Jer 16:17
[b]Ps 19:12; Eccl 12:14

Psalm 90:9
[1]Or *whisper*
[a]Ps 78:33

Psalm 90:10
[1]Lit *years*
[2]Lit *in them are*
[a]2 Kin 19:35
[b]Eccl 12:2-7; Jer 20:18
[c]Job 20:8; Ps 78:39

Psalm 90:11
[1]Or *knows*
[2]Lit *of You*
[a]Ps 76:7
[b]Neh 5:9

Psalm 90:12
[1]Or *gain, bring in*
[a]Deut 32:29; Ps 39:4
[b]Prov 2:1-6

Psalm 90:13
[1]Or *repent in regard to*
[a]Ps 6:4; 80:14
[b]Ps 6:3; 74:10
[c]Ex 32:12; Deut 32:36; Ps 106:45; 135:14; Amos 7:3, 6; Jon 3:9

Psalm 90:14
[a]Ps 36:8; 65:4; 103:5; Jer 31:14
[b]Ps 31:7; 85:6

Psalm 90:15
[1]Or *as many days as*

[2]Or *trouble*
[a]Ps 86:4
[b]Deut 2:14-16; Ps 31:10

Psalm 90:16

[1]Or *upon*
[a]Deut 32:4; Ps 44:1; 77:12; 92:4; Hab 3:2
[b]1 Kin 8:11; Is 6:3

Psalm 90:17

[1]Or *give permanence to*
[a]Ps 27:4
[b]Ps 37:23; Is 26:12; 1 Cor 3:7

Targum

Psa. 90:1 The prayer that Moses the prophet of the LORD prayed when the people, the house of Israel, sinned in the wilderness. He raised his voice and thus he said: O LORD, the dwelling of whose presence is in heaven, you have been for us a helper in every generation. **2** When it was manifest in your presence that your people were going to sin, you established repentance; before ever the mountains were lifted up and the earth and the world's inhabitants created, and from this age to the age to come, you are God. **3** You will return a son of man to death because of his sin; and [yet] you have said, "Repent, O sons of men." **4** For a thousand years in your eyes are considered in your presence like a yesterday, for it will pass; and like a watch in the night. **5** And if they do not repent, death will come upon them, they will be as those who are sleeping; and in the age to come, they will disappear like crumbling grass. [ANOTHER TARGUM: You made them drink the cup of cursing; they became like a drunken man in his sleep.] **6** Their deeds are like grass that in the morning will spring up and multiply; in the evening it fades and dries up from the heat. **7** For we have been destroyed by your harshness, and by your anger we have been terrified. **8** You have set our sins in front of you, the iniquities of our youth before the light of your face. **9** For all our days have been removed from your presence in your anger; we have completed the days of our lives like a vapor of the mouth in winter. **10** The days of our years in this age are seventy years, quickly passing; and if [one is] in strength, eighty years; but most of them are toil and deceit for the guilty, for they pass in haste and fly away to the morning. **11** Who is he who knows how to turn back the force of your harshness? – except the righteous, who fear you, appease your anger. **12** Who is right to teach us to number our days, except the prophet, whose heart pours forth wisdom? **13** Turn, O LORD – how long will you afflict us? – and turn from the harm that you commanded to do to your servants. **14** Satisfy us with your goodness in the age that is likened to a morning, and we will rejoice and be glad in all our days. **15** Gladden us like the days that you afflicted us, like the years that we saw harm. **16** Let the works of your miracles appear to your servants, and let your splendor be upon their sons. **17** And may the pleasantness of the Garden of Eden be upon us from the presence of the LORD our God, and the works of our hands will be established by him.

Spiritual Awareness

Introduction

This Psalm starts the fourth book of the Psalms. The first eleven works of the fourth book were composed by Moses. The sage Rashi explains that these Psalms were Moses's blessings on eleven tribes. Simeon was excluded from the blessings because they held an orgy (Numbers 25:1-15). The sage Radak explained that David found these eleven Psalms in an old manuscript to which the authorship of Moses had traditionally been ascribed. David decided to adapt these Psalms into his book of Psalms.

Verse five

The LORD will often allow a thousand years to stream away like raindrops on the earth. It is a process of regeneration and restoration. When it is over, there is a renewed vigor like a fresh young sprout of grass.

You let them flow away; sleep they become, but in the morning, it renews its vigor fresh as grass.

Verse 12

All the happiness humans can live in comes from the blissful certainty that they have lived all their years, days, hours, and minutes on earth in loyalty to the LORD.

So teach us to number our days, then we shall bring home a heart of wisdom.

Verse fourteen

Satisfy us with the loving-kindness of the Sefirah Chesed in the morning; then, we shall exult and be glad in our days.

APPENDIX

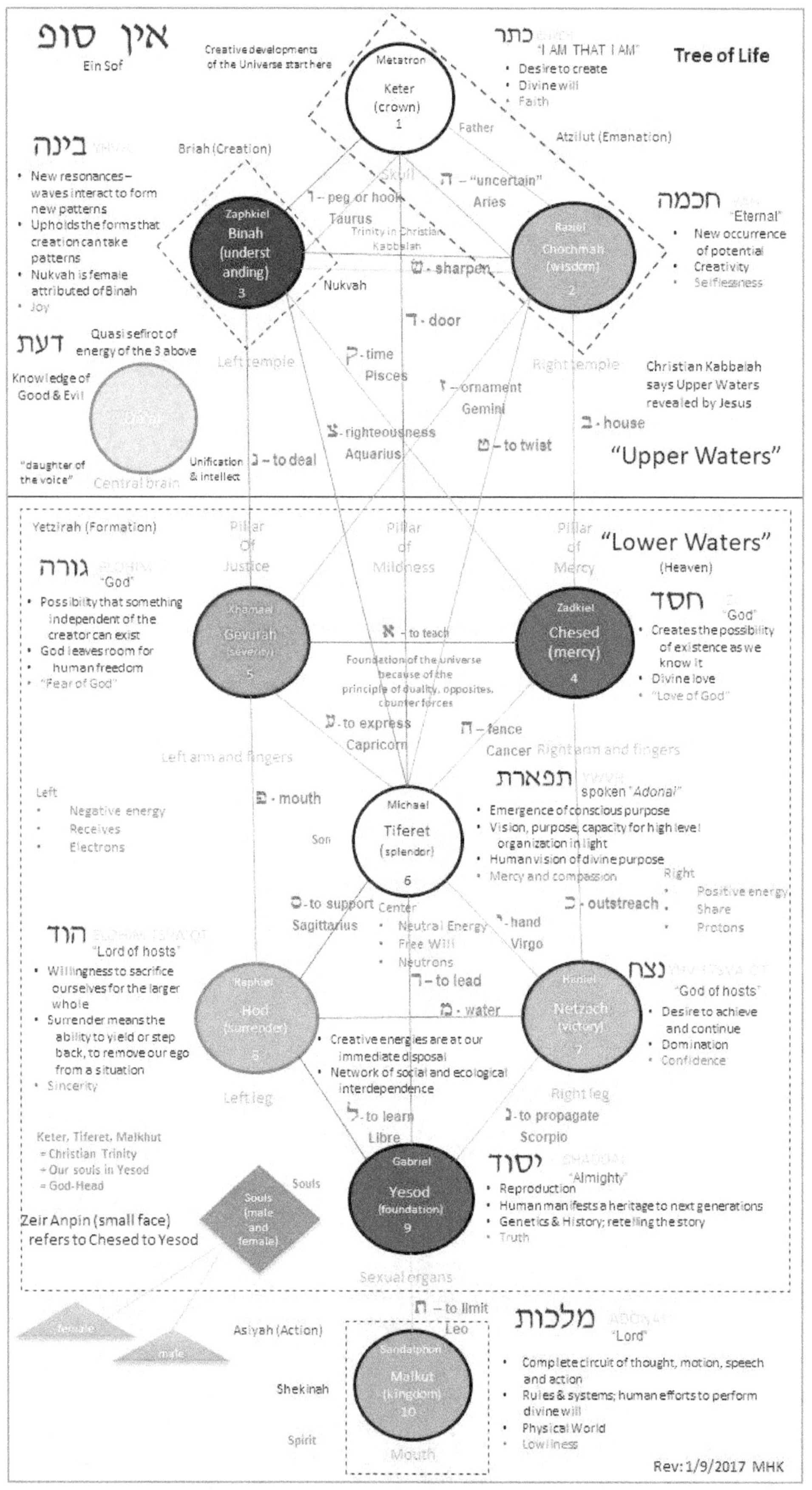
אין סוף
Ein Sof

Tree of Life

כתר
"I AM THAT I AM"
• Desire to create
• Divine will
• Faith

Creative developments of the Universe start here

Metatron
Keter
(crown)
1

Father

Atzilut (Emanation)

בינה
• New resonances—waves interact to form new patterns
• Upholds the forms that creation can take patterns
• Nukvah is female attributed of Binah
• Joy

Briah (Creation)

ו -- peg or hook
Taurus

ה – "uncertain"
Aries

Trinity in Christian Kabbalah

חכמה
"Eternal"
• New occurrence of potential
• Creativity
• Selflessness

Zaphkiel
Binah
(understanding)
3

ש - sharpen

Raziel
Chochmah
(wisdom)
2

Nukvah

ד - door

דעת
Quasi sefirot of energy of the 3 above

Knowledge of Good & Evil

ק - time
Pisces

Christian Kabbalah says Upper Waters revealed by Jesus

Left temple

ז – ornament
Gemini

Right temple

Da'at

צ - righteousness
Aquarius

ב - house

"daughter of the voice"

Central brain

Unification & intellect

ג – to deal

ט – to twist

"Upper Waters"

Yetzirah (Formation)

Pillar Of Justice

Pillar of Mildness

Pillar of Mercy

"Lower Waters"
(Heaven)

גורה
"God"
• Possibility that something independent of the creator can exist
• God leaves room for human freedom
• "Fear of God"

Khamael
Gevurah
(severity)
5

א - to teach

Zadkiel
Chesed
(mercy)
4

חסד
"God"
• Creates the possibility of existence as we know it
• Divine love
• "Love of God"

Foundation of the universe because of the principle of duality, opposites, counter forces

ע - to express
Capricorn

ח – fence
Cancer

Left arm and fingers

Right arm and fingers

Left
• Negative energy
• Receives
• Electrons

פ - mouth

תפארת
spoken "Adonai"
• Emergence of conscious purpose
• Vision, purpose, capacity for high level organization in light
• Human vision of divine purpose
• Mercy and compassion

Michael
Tiferet
(splendor)
6

Son

Right

כ - outstreach

Positive energy
Share
Protons

ס - to support
Sagittarius

Center
• Neutral Energy
• Free Will
• Neutrons

י - hand
Virgo

הוד
"Lord of hosts"
• Willingness to sacrifice ourselves for the larger whole
• Surrender means the ability to yield or step back, to remove our ego from a situation
• Sincerity

ר - to lead

מ - water

נצח
"God of hosts"
• Desire to achieve and continue
• Domination
• Confidence

Raphiel
Hod
(surrender)
8

Haniel
Netzach
(victory)
7

Left leg

Right leg

Keter, Tiferet, Malkhut
= Christian Trinity
+ Our souls in Yesod
= God-Head

Zeir Anpin (small face) refers to Chesed to Yesod

ל - to learn
Libre

נ - to propagate
Scorpio

Souls (male and female)

Souls

Gabriel
Yesod
(foundation)
9

יסוד
"Almighty"
• Reproduction
• Human manifests a heritage to next generations
• Genetics & History; retelling the story
• Truth

Sexual organs

female

male

Asiyah (Action)

ת – to limit
Leo

מלכות
"Lord"

Shekinah

Sandalphon
Malkut
(kingdom)
10

• Complete circuit of thought, motion, speech and action
• Rules & systems; human efforts to perform divine will
• Physical World
• Lowliness

Spirit

Mouth

Rev: 1/9/2017 MHK

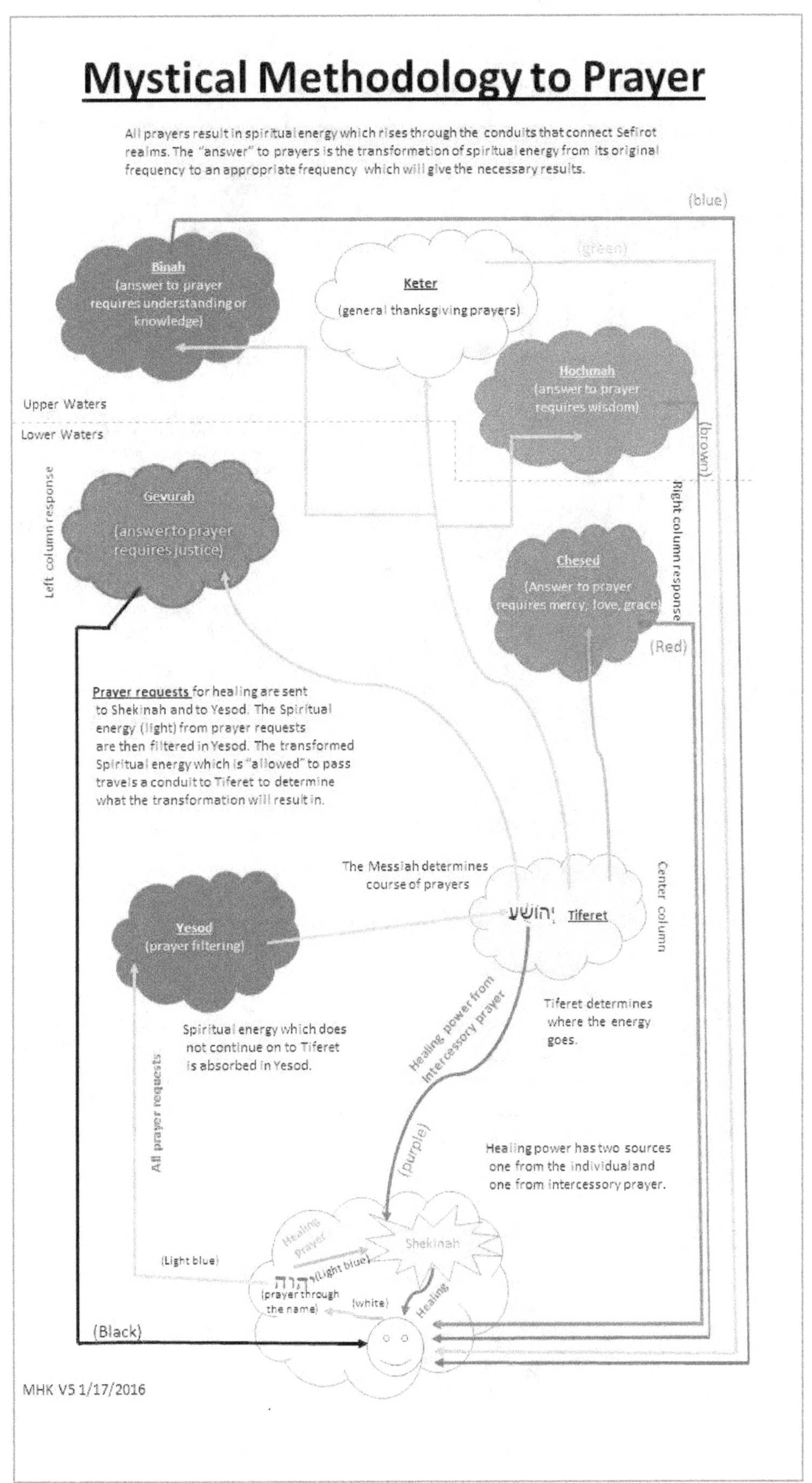

Mystical Methodology to Prayer
All prayers result in spiritual energy which rises through the conduits that connect Sefirot realms. The "answer" to prayers is the transformation of spiritual energy from its original frequency to an appropriate frequency which will give the necessary results.
(blue)
(green)
Binah
(answer to prayer requires understanding or knowledge)
Keter
(general thanksgiving prayers)
Hochmah
(answer to prayer requires wisdom)
Upper Waters
Lower Waters
(brown)
Left column response
Gevurah
(answer to prayer requires justice)
Right column response
Chesed
(Answer to prayer requires mercy, love, grace)
(Red)
Prayer requests for healing are sent to Shekinah and to Yesod. The Spiritual energy (light) from prayer requests are then filtered in Yesod. The transformed Spiritual energy which is "allowed" to pass travels a conduit to Tiferet to determine what the transformation will result in.
The Messiah determines course of prayers
יהושע Tiferet
Center column
Yesod
(prayer filtering)
Spiritual energy which does not continue on to Tiferet is absorbed in Yesod.
Healing power from Intercessory prayer
Tiferet determines where the energy goes.
All prayer requests
(purple)
Healing power has two sources one from the individual and one from intercessory prayer.
(Light blue)
Healing prayer
(Light blue)
Shekinah
יהוה
(prayer through the name)
(white)
Healing
(Black)
MHK V5 1/17/2016

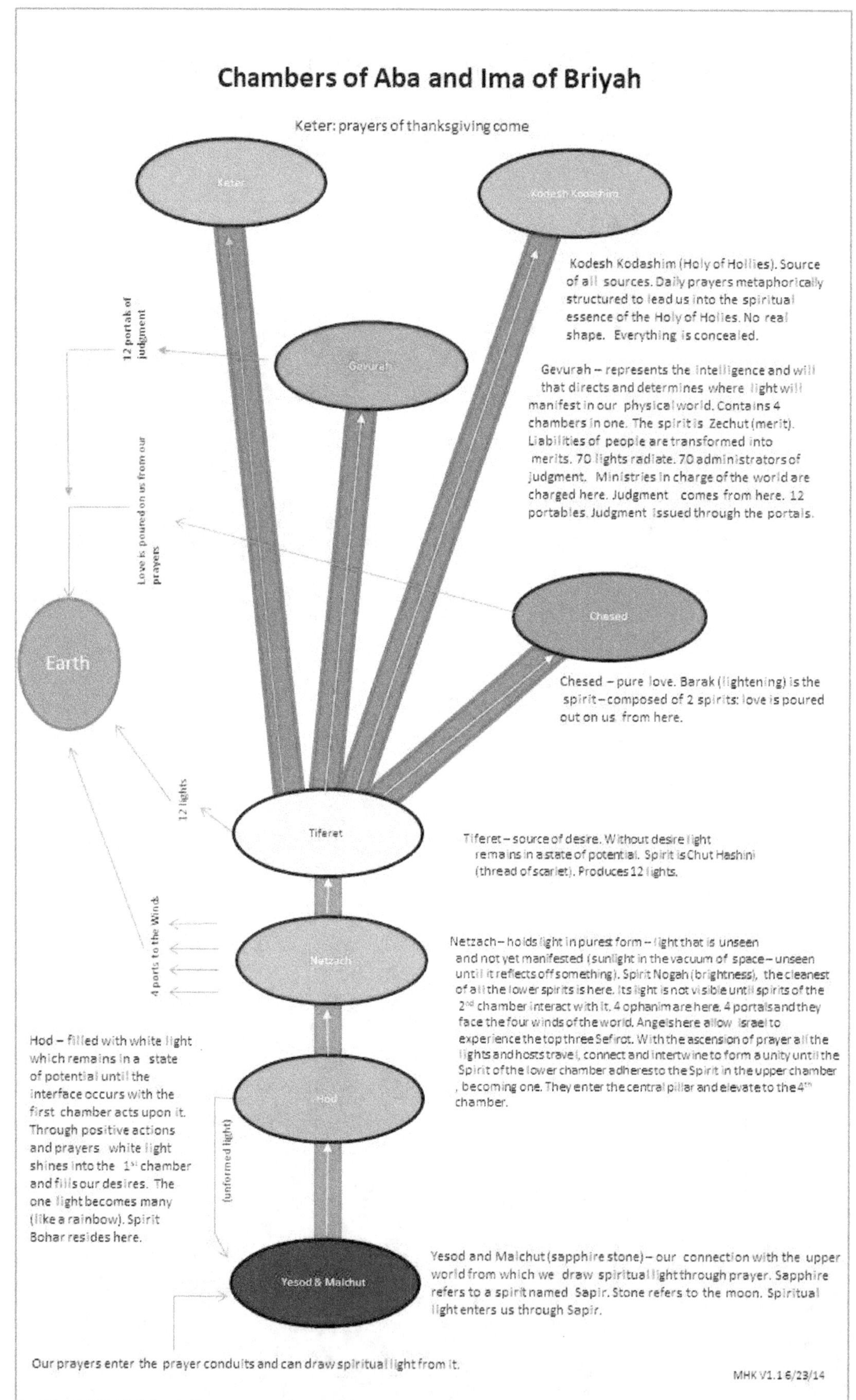

Chambers of Aba and Ima of Briyah
Keter: prayers of thanksgiving come
Keter
Kodesh Kodashim
Gevurah
Earth
12 portals of judgment
Love is poured on us from our prayers
Chesed
Tiferet
12 lights
Netzach
4 ports to the Winds
Hod
(unformed light)
Yesod & Malchut
Kodesh Kodashim (Holy of Hollies). Source of all sources. Daily prayers metaphorically structured to lead us into the spiritual essence of the Holy of Holies. No real shape. Everything is concealed.
Gevurah – represents the intelligence and will that directs and determines where light will manifest in our physical world. Contains 4 chambers in one. The spirit is Zechut (merit). Liabilities of people are transformed into merits. 70 lights radiate. 70 administrators of judgment. Ministries in charge of the world are charged here. Judgment comes from here. 12 portables. Judgment issued through the portals.
Chesed – pure love. Barak (lightening) is the spirit – composed of 2 spirits: love is poured out on us from here.
Tiferet – source of desire. Without desire light remains in a state of potential. Spirit is Chut Hashini (thread of scarlet). Produces 12 lights.
Netzach – holds light in purest form – light that is unseen and not yet manifested (sunlight in the vacuum of space – unseen until it reflects off something). Spirit Nogah (brightness), the cleanest of all the lower spirits is here. Its light is not visible until spirits of the 2nd chamber interact with it. 4 ophanim are here. 4 portals and they face the four winds of the world. Angels here allow Israel to experience the top three Sefirot. With the ascension of prayer all the lights and hosts travel, connect and intertwine to form a unity until the Spirit of the lower chamber adheres to the Spirit in the upper chamber, becoming one. They enter the central pillar and elevate to the 4th chamber.
Hod – filled with white light which remains in a state of potential until the interface occurs with the first chamber acts upon it. Through positive actions and prayers white light shines into the 1st chamber and fills our desires. The one light becomes many (like a rainbow). Spirit Bohar resides here.
Yesod and Malchut (sapphire stone) – our connection with the upper world from which we draw spiritual light through prayer. Sapphire refers to a spirit named Sapir. Stone refers to the moon. Spiritual light enters us through Sapir.
Our prayers enter the prayer conduits and can draw spiritual light from it.
MHK V1.1 6/23/14

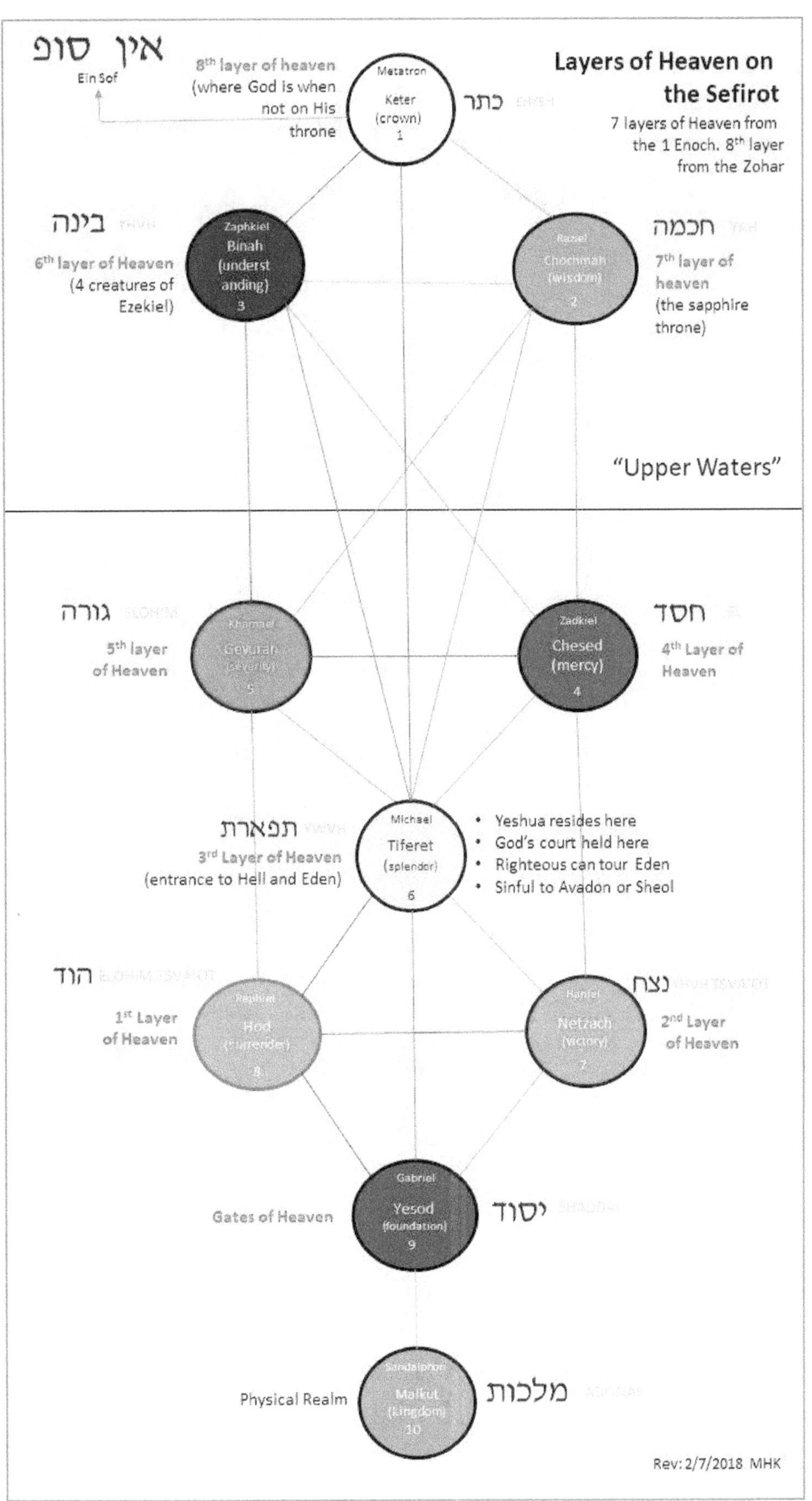
אין סוף
Ein Sof
8th layer of heaven (where God is when not on His throne)
Metatron
Keter (crown)
1
כתר
Layers of Heaven on the Sefirot
7 layers of Heaven from the 1 Enoch. 8th layer from the Zohar
בינה
6th layer of Heaven (4 creatures of Ezekiel)
Zaphkiel
Binah (understanding)
3
חכמה
Raziel
Chochmah (wisdom)
2
7th layer of heaven (the sapphire throne)
"Upper Waters"
גורה
5th layer of Heaven
Khamael
Gevurah (severity)
5
Zadkiel
Chesed (mercy)
4
חסד
4th Layer of Heaven
תפארת
3rd Layer of Heaven (entrance to Hell and Eden)
Michael
Tiferet (splendor)
6
• Yeshua resides here
• God's court held here
• Righteous can tour Eden
• Sinful to Avadon or Sheol
הוד
1st Layer of Heaven
Raphael
Hod (Surrender)
8
Haniel
Netzach (victory)
7
נצח
2nd Layer of Heaven
Gates of Heaven
Gabriel
Yesod (foundation)
9
יסוד
Physical Realm
Sandalphon
Malkut (kingdom)
10
מלכות
Rev: 2/7/2018 MHK

94